The Masculine
Journey

T H E

MASCULINE JOURNEY

UNDERSTANDING THE SIX STAGES OF MANHOOD

ROBERT HICKS

NAVPRESS

BRINGING TRUTH TO LIFE
NavPress Publishing Group
P.O. Box 35001, Colorado Springs, Colorado 80935

The Navigators is an international Christian organization. Jesus Christ gave His followers the Great
Commission to go and make disciples (Matthew
28:19). The aim of The Navigators is to help fulfill
that commission by multiplying laborers for Christ in
every nation.

NavPress is the publishing ministry of The Navigators.
NavPress publications are tools to help Christians
grow. Although publications alone cannot make disciples or change lives, they can help believers learn
biblical discipleship, and apply what they learn to their
lives and ministries.

© 1993 by Robert Hicks
All rights reserved. No part of this publication may
     be reproduced in any form without written per-
     mission from NavPress, P.O. Box 35001, Colorado
     Springs, CO 80935.
Library of Congress Catalog Card Number:
     93-4042
ISBN 08910-97333

Some of the anecdotal illustrations in this book are
true to life and are included with the permission of the
persons involved. All other illustrations are composites
of real situations, and any resemblance to people living
or dead is coincidental.

Unless otherwise identified, all Scripture quotations
in this publication are taken from the *New American
Standard Bible* (NASB), © The Lockman Foundation 1960,
1962, 1963, 1968, 1971, 1972, 1973, 1975, 1977. Another
version used is the *HOLY BIBLE: NEW INTERNA-
TIONAL VERSION*® (NIV®), Copyright © 1973, 1978,
1984 by International Bible Society, used by permission
of Zondervan Publishing House, all rights reserved.

Hicks, Robert, 1945-
     The masculine journey : understanding the six
stages of manhood / Robert Hicks.
         p.   cm.
     Includes bibliographical references.
     ISBN 0-89109-733-3
     1. Men—Psychology. 2. Masculinity (Psychology)
3. Men (Christian theology) 4. Men—Religious
life. I.   Title.
BF692.5.H525   1993
155.3'32—dc20   93-4042
                                                 CIP

Printed in the United States of America

FOR A FREE CATALOG OF
NAVPRESS BOOKS & BIBLE STUDIES,
CALL 1-800-366-7788 (USA)
or 1-416-499-4615 (CANADA)

Contents

◆

To Graham

My namesake, my companion,
my brother in arms, my guy —
for your journey as a man,
this book is for you.

As an M-16 in the hands of a marine,
so are you, the son of my youth.[1]

I am a father singularly blessed.

Foreword

◆

If there's one universal complaint that many of our wives and daughters have against us, it's summed up in the words, "He won't stop for directions!"

And it's true! For many men, stopping to ask for directions is a sign of weakness. The important thing is to keep the car moving — past every roadside rest and gas station — even if we're making great time going down the wrong road.

Being lost on vacation can become a funny memory after a few months. But many of us are facing something much more serious. With the cultural confusion that has taken place over the past fifty years, a whole generation of men like us have gotten lost on the way to finding ourselves, our purpose, and our mission in life.

Perhaps you've felt lost at times on your masculine journey. I certainly have. I grew up in a single-parent home with my older brother and twin brother. I was only three months old when my father left, and my mother would never remarry. That left three boys under three to begin a journey toward manhood that included frequent stops at the television, mistaken peers, and misguided role models.

I wish I'd had a copy of this book when I was a young man, grappling with what biblical masculinity really was. I'm thankful that I have it now, when it's still easy to follow a misguided world, and end up lost and alone.

In *The Masculine Journey* Robert Hicks shares a developmental journey to help you understand the way the Bible views masculinity. By looking closely at the six words the Old Testament frequently uses to define a man's journey, you'll find insight and understanding for whatever season of life you're in. Whether you're a young man, defining yourself by your strength; in middle age, fighting to build correct priorities; or in your later years, seeking to stay the course, there's wisdom and encouragement here for you.

But don't look for easy answers or simple formulas. This book is a meaty challenge that will stretch you in all the right ways. By investing the time to look closely at these six words, you'll be rewarded by learning important principles to help you understand your strength, sexuality, and sorrows.

In the infantry, you don't move up the ranks without becoming proficient at map reading—a skill that takes time and concentration. Yet the time spent mastering the map pays off when the battle is raging. When an officer or non-com calls in an artillery or air strike, he better be sure of his coordinates. Many lives hang in the balance, and the battle may be won or lost according to whether he has read the map correctly.

So it is in our homes today. How many of us are lost when it comes to really understanding what masculinity is? And our unwillingness to stop and ask for directions is putting us and our families at risk. But God's Word provides a light for our path. In some ways, it gives us a masculine map, fleshed out in these key, biblical words that point us toward what we're called to be—men of God. It will leave you with insights that can change your life, and mine, for the better.

JOHN TRENT, PH.D.
Author, national conference speaker,
and president of Encouraging Words,
a nationwide ministry to men and their families
based in Phoenix, Arizona

Acknowledgments

◆

Thanks goes to NavPress and the Promise Keepers for having a vision for this project. I greatly appreciate their commitment to men and the publishing of materials that relate directly to men's issues.

Thanks goes to my friends of the Men's Breakfast Club at the Church of the Savior, Wayne, Pennsylvania. You were my sounding board for many of the issues addressed in this book. Thank you for your honest sharing and faithful attendance for the almost five years I was with you.

A hearty thank you also goes to the owners of my two retreat homes. Bob and Debbie Blum, your place at the Jersey shore continues to be the perfect place to slip off to and write to meet deadlines. Your generosity is neither forgotten nor left unacknowledged. To my mother-in-love, Ann Rosenburg, your Blowing Rock mountain home made the completion of this book *on time* possible. I could not have finished it without having a place to slip off to during the holidays when this book was due.

Thanks goes to my newfound friend and fellow guitar-picker, Steve Griffith. This project could not have been possible without your belief in me and your tenacity to not only find a publisher but the right publisher. Thanks for putting the project together.

Thanks and apology go to my family. Little did I know when I agreed to a completion date on this book that my daughter Charis would be getting a ring for Christmas with a February wedding date. The surprise put Cinny into the hectic time of making wedding plans with her husband off in the mountains. Every day I felt guilty about being away during this time, but my family's encouragement and understanding kept me writing. Without their love and support there would be no masculine journey. Graham and Ashley, I appreciate the liberality you extended your father in missing a major slice of holiday vacation time. Charis (now a wonderfully married lady), as my firstborn about to leave the nest, I am most proud to give you away to Jason, and be able to perform the ceremony as well.

Finally, I give thanks and credit to the one who has lived with me for the last twenty-something years. Cinny, is the one who has both watched and walked with me in this thing called the masculine journey. I only wish I could enter her feminine world as well as she has entered and understood this masculine one. Thank you for the patience, understanding, and commitment you have shown to this one man on his masculine journey.

CHAPTER ONE

An Uneasy Men's Movement

◆

*The longest journey
Is the journey inwards
Of him who has chosen his destiny.*

DAG HAMMARSKJÖLD
Quoted in *Bartlett's Familiar Quotations*

I GET LOST . . . often. Where I live, many of the roads are over two hundred years old, and there exists no logic as to why they run the way they do. I moved to this area near historic Valley Forge from the Dallas–Fort Worth area. There the roads run straight and predictable. Municipal planners obviously laid out those cities. But not so here. The only sensible way for a newcomer to get oriented to the area and find his way around is with a map. But for some unknown reason, I hate maps. They take all the challenge out of life. Asking directions would seem logical. But that also takes much of the adventure out of finding one's destination. Besides, at most of the places where I stop and ask directions, people just give me a strange look and say something like, "I'm not from around here." So, I try to do it on my own, and I get lost.

My experience, I have come to learn, is part and parcel

with the masculine experience. Men don't like to ask for directions. But we desperately need directions for our respective journeys. Without directions we end up lost. Whether as developing teenagers, midlife males, or senior mentors, men need a kind of map that will trace the masculine journey — a map that shows us what's up ahead, and how we are to get from one point to another. *The Masculine Journey* tries to reveal this male developmental journey and provide directions for a man's life so that he doesn't get lost along the way. In this sense, this book is a sequel to my previous work on men's issues.

Since the publication of my book *Uneasy Manhood*, much has happened in the men's movement. In fact, while writing that book, I was not even aware of a movement. I wrote out of my own experience as a man and from my interaction with other men I knew. By the time the book appeared almost every major news magazine and television talk show had published articles and aired programs discussing the growing awareness of men's issues. Often, the tone of the discussion was tongue in cheek, and the movement was treated in a less-than-serious way. Even Murphy Brown pooh-poohed men going out into the woods, beating drums, and getting in touch with nature and themselves.

Despite the press, men are openly reading and discussing new male topics in an attempt to rediscover something that they feel has been lost. Sam Keen has encouraged us to find the "fire in the belly";[1] Robert Bly, to find the "wild man within us."[2] Jungian psychologists argue for finding or rediscovering the primitive archetypes lost in most men. Robert Johnson puts us on a search for the lost feminine,[3] and Sam Osherson urges us to reconnect with our lost fathers.[4] Deborah Tannen has told us that we speak and hear different languages,[5] and Warren Farrell just makes us mad by revealing that despite all the talk about the gender revolution, both men and women have remained firmly rooted to their primary fantasies.[6]

For most men all this discussion is fairly high sounding and theoretical. What they really want to know is, What does it mean to be a man? The women in their lives want to know

as well. In fact, it would seem today that women are as confused about this thing called *maleness* as the men are. Many
say they want sensitivity in men but then turn around and say
the sensitive, caring male is nothing but a wimp. Underneath,
there seems to be a gnawing realization among men that what
women really want from men is the same old thing—for us to
be strong, aggressive, and of course, successful!

When an author writes a book, he doesn't know what
paths the book will open up. This was certainly true in my
case. The response to my book *Uneasy Manhood* has been more
than gratifying to me as an author. However, one path the book
placed me on was the radio and television talk-show circuit.
Since the publication of the book in 1991, I've done over 150
radio and television interviews based on the book or on men's
issues. From this experience, I have learned where many of the
gaps in my thinking have been. In *Uneasy Manhood*, my goal
was to explore for my readers the areas of uneasiness among
men. I worked on the premise that all was not well with men
in our American society. Men were not doing as well as often
perceived by women. Because most men don't talk at the feeling level, most women just think everything is fine with them,
or worse, that men don't have any feelings at all!

However, on the talk-show circuit one has to interact
face to face with one's audience. You can't put them off.
They question you, show you the areas you haven't given
adequate thought to. Such was the case on one nationwide
program. I thought I had done a fairly good job explaining
the uneasiness of men to the program host (a woman). As is
customary for these shows, guests can receive a videotape of
the program, for a fee of course. Having obtained a copy, I sat
down and watched myself on the tape. What I saw disturbed
me. At one point in the interview, the host asked me, "So
what is a man?" As I watched myself answer her question,
it became very apparent to me (I hope not to the viewers) that
I didn't have a clue! I saw myself backpedaling, quoting other
writers, avoiding making any definitive statement that might
be viewed as not "politically correct" by our feminist-aware

culture. In short, I realized that I had written an entire book on men's issues without addressing *the* most fundamental issue among men and women: What is a man?

The question is fundamentally simple. But the answer, especially today in the wake of feminist equalitarianism, is not only difficult but virtually impossible. As I began thinking about my reading and research in the field, I wasn't satisfied with most of the "expert" definitions. The Jungian writers and counselors assert that to be a real man today is to find our feminine spirits (anima) that have been lying dormant within us. This has sold well among feminists because it places the emphasis on men finding their softer side and becoming more nurturing. Now, I'm certainly not opposed to men becoming more nurturing, but what I react to is the assumption in the theory.

This assumption surfaced during an enlightening panel discussion at an eastern university. A panel was put together by the women's studies department. The panel included three women and me, the sole representative of the male gender. The announced title was "Men and Women in Relationship." However, I sensed very quickly that the agenda was far more feminine than masculine. One of the panel members was a Jungian psychotherapist. She was setting forth the theoretical basis for male and female relationships based on Carl Jung's understanding of the animus/anima dynamic within both genders. She concluded by saying, "The only hope for men in moving beyond the violence and aggression of their older role is to discover the female spirit (anima) within them."

I could hold my tongue no longer. As kindly as I could put it (one must be sensitive in such situations!), I asked, "How do you know for a fact that there *is* a feminine spirit inside every man?" I thought it was a fairly simple question for a Jungian analyst. I was merely trying to find out whether there was a sufficient research base, or some psychobiological studies, to affirm such a conclusion. As I watched the entire audience (mostly female) move their eyes and heads to the other end of the table, I noticed that my fellow panelist looked a little perplexed. Finally she admitted, "I guess I've never really thought about that!" I responded, "I would think it important that, before we put men or women on a search for something, we know it is there to be found." I have known men who have started down that road of the psychic-feminine-within, only to find that it led nowhere, or to the discovery of something they already knew—that they were men!

So the Jungian definition of manhood doesn't work for me. But where else do we go? Well, Robert Bly goes to mythology. The title of his book is based on its main character, Iron John, who is taken from one of Hans Christian Andersen's fairy tales. Iron John is a hairy man who lives on the bottom of a pond, and who becomes the mentor of a young boy in search of his manhood. Of course, the goal of becoming a man is to find the Iron John within us—the wild man who lives in the forest of our lives. Now I must admit, at least at the experiential level, I find more of the wild man within me than the feminine spirit. Therefore, I find Iron John more attractive than looking for the holy grail of my *anima* (female spirit). However, I still have some theoretical problems in basing an entire philosophy of manhood on fables. Even though I understand that there exists a consistent reappearance of male themes or archetypes throughout primitive literature, this is not to say that they are authoritative enough to base human or masculine nature upon.

These are the more recent nonreligious attempts to define manhood in terms other than those of the pre- and post-feminist eras. The pre-feminist 1950s saw the real man as John Wayne, the strong-quiet type. The post-feminist era placed more emphasis on the Alan Alda type, the sensitive-nurturing male. In an interesting switch, during this politically correct sensitive-male era, we have seen a major return to the John Wayne strong-silent type. What else do the Sly Stallones, Arnold Schwarzeneggers, Norman Schwarzkopfs, and Steven Seagals illustrate? Add to these the Donald Trumps, Ted Turners, and Ross Perots, and we see an interesting conflict between what much of the literature says about the way men ought to be, and who we honor with our money, time, and fantasy images.

So it seems the answers to my question about defining a

man are many. Is the true man one who has found his feminine side, or his wild man? Is he the strong male, the sensitive male, or the successful-in-business male? Or is true manhood just plain celluloid that doesn't really exist anywhere except in our fantasies?

In *Uneasy Manhood*, the closest I came to defining manhood was in my last chapter. Writing as a pastoral theologian in the evangelical tradition, I looked to Jesus as the model of manhood for which men should strive. In the life of Jesus what can be seen is the unique integration of both strength and sensitivity. Many men in our generation are either all strength or all sensitivity. Each suffers a serious deficiency of normative male experience. The macho male needs to develop sensitivity. The sensitive male of the sixties needs to discover his strength, to find the wild man and the fire in his belly! I believe the model of Jesus provides a very helpful visual image for men who study His life in its completeness and without the modern stereotypes that are often thrust upon the biblical accounts. To let the gospel accounts of Jesus speak for themselves is one of the most difficult tasks. Some want to strip away anything that doesn't fit our present culture. Feminists do this when they only comment on the sensitivity of Jesus. Others don't see any relevance to Jesus as a model of manhood at all. Even Bly sees Jesus as a very weak male who only modeled passivity. He prefers John the Baptist, a hairy wild man, over Jesus.[7]

In my presentation of manhood in *Uneasy Manhood*, I did not detail how the model of Jesus can be seen throughout the lengthy adult life cycle for men. The dynamics of both strength and sensitivity change as men get older. As I watched myself on that talk-show video, I realized that I was not clear enough on how manhood can be defined differently through the life cycle. What I saw concerned me.

A few weeks later I was flying from Philadelphia to Memphis to speak at a men's conference. I had been asked to do a seminar on the issues addressed in my book. As I sat on the plane reviewing my notes, I concluded I didn't like my approach. The television interview haunted me. "What is a man?" The question continued to roll over and over in my mind. I thought of the men's literature, my book, the men I knew, and the tensions in my own life about being a man in midlife.

Then I remembered a book about men I had read years before the men's movement was in vogue. It was still in my opinion the critical work that offered an excellent research base, and was true to the reality I had experienced as a man. It was Daniel Levinson's book *The Seasons of a Man's Life.*[8] Levinson looks in depth at the lives of forty men and from this research draws a theoretical developmental frame for understanding what manhood is all about. His conclusions were simple: Manhood is reflected differently throughout the adult life cycle. There exist certain predictable eras in the male life cycle.[9] This structure appealed to me because it fit my experience and the experience of so many other men, but I needed to be more convinced.

As a biblically trained theologian I asked, "Do the Scriptures have anything to contribute in this regard?" I took the pen from my inside coat pocket, turned my drink napkin over, and amidst the dispersing of in-flight meals, began to scribble some generally unrecognizable scrawls on the napkin. Six words of ancient origin came back to me from my educational experience. I uttered a silent "Thank You, God" for, of all things, Hebrew 101! My Hebrew prof told me I could use this some day!

Here they were: six words for "man" learned in Hebrew class years earlier, now shedding the light I needed to speak to the men during the weekend. It was also the light I wish I would have had that day on the talk show. The words on the napkin written in Hebrew (backwards from the English way of writing) and looking more like chicken scratches, provided me with a biblical framework that was both descriptive of the long-standing male experience throughout the centuries and also true to the current literature. The words also seem to reflect the same seasonal or developmental aspects that have been demonstrated in so many of the recent men's studies. In this sense they provided a map — a set of directions or stages for men — a way for defining and detailing the masculine experience. Maps always show us the way, and define for us where the journey will take us in an attempt to keep us from becoming lost. Many men have found themselves lost in this maze called life because they have not had adequate guidance.

What this book attempts to lay out for men is *one* way of looking at the masculine journey. In this sense, the book is descriptive and not necessarily prescriptive. It is always tempting to move from observation to exhortation, from what is to what ought to be. This is not only a logical fallacy but also downright dangerous. The journey that I am attempting to define is one drawn from the usage of six predominant Hebrew words that create concepts about the masculine journey. I do not claim to be a linguist, especially not one of the Semitic kind. However, I have tried to give ample evidence in the notes at the end of the chapters for the common usage and derivation of the words.

For my more critical readers who desire to know if I can prove my arguments, the references will hopefully give the information needed to check sources. I have also consulted my friend, colleague, and Semitics professor, Dr. John Worgul (Ph.D. in Semitic Studies, Dropsie College), on the fine points of biblical word-study meanings. As one noted for his "motif" approach to theology, he has encouraged me greatly in supporting the primary usages of these terms. As in any language, words do not always have the same meaning in every context, therefore the meaning I ascribe to each of these words is not necessarily universal. However, these words, as I am using them, do say something very descriptive and normative about the masculine experience, which in turn helps us to delineate the meaning of manhood.

The Developmental Journey

One of the major contributions of Levinson's work was applying to men the reality that adult life is not static. It is a journey, and while on a journey the landscape is constantly changing. This reality still seems to surprise many men. We expect our jobs, our marriages, even our faith to mean the same things as we get older. When we see changes in ourselves we think something is seriously wrong, rather than recognizing this is a normal part of the journey. Being on a trip means there are always new beginnings and saying goodbye to old friends. Terminations, starting again, detours, speeding up, and slowing down are all normal parts of the trip. So it is with adult life. Also, being on a journey means that every new encounter demands some appropriate response or adjustment. Traveling from the American South to the more northern areas demands a change in the type of clothing, or even a change in expectations about how people behave toward one another. Nashville is not Philadelphia, and New York is not Dallas! Likewise, western Pennsylvania is not like eastern Pennsylvania — the former being more midwestern while the latter more typically eastern.

This is not to say that one place is better than another. They are just different, and these differences demand certain adjustments.

So it is in understanding adult male development. One particular stage or season on the male journey is not the only "real man" place. Each stage, or station, reflects something about what it means to be masculine at that stage of a man's life. What characterizes and defines a man in his twenties is not the same as what may characterize and define a man in his forties. But both are stages of manhood, and knowing what is appropriate for each season is important. What a man experiences and should be in his forties, as compared to his twenties or sixties, is all part of being a man. These stages all make up the normative masculine experience.

I know some readers may react to using a phrase like "normative masculine experience." We have been led to believe that in the area of gender, nothing anymore is normative. However, as this book and my former book have sought to demonstrate, this idea is pure modern fiction. There exist critical differences between men and women in almost every conceivable area.[10] But in the absence of fathers and older male mentors in our culture, mixed with the dominance of feminine definitions and expectations about maleness, it is not socially or politically correct to talk about the normative male. I believe there *is* a normative male, which is depicted in the following pages, as illustrated by the six Hebrew words we'll study, and which has been validated by contemporary men's issue research.

Understanding these six stages as a journey also suggests that at every new place encountered there is a time of *separation* from the past, *initiation* to something new, *transition* from one place to the other, and temporary *confusion*. These will become very important concepts to bear in mind throughout the book. At every season of life these developmental tasks are required in order to keep moving on the journey without getting lost or stuck in the developmental mud! In some cases these required tasks will be very intentional and predictable.

When a man marries he intentionally places himself in a situation that will require some adjustment and change. In this sense, the transition period is predictable. His separation from his parents and the single lifestyle and initiation into married life creates a certain confusion for a time—this is normative and very predictable. However, when the same young man loses his job in his first year of marriage, he faces another kind of separation, initiation, transition, and confusion. This one is not expected, is unpredictable, and seems inappropriate for the season he is in. Therefore, this adjustment and transition may be harder and longer, but the experience just the same is normative for a man. The season of wounding is perhaps "out of sync" in the young man's mind, but it is nevertheless a rich aspect of the male experience and one from which he will learn much about himself and manhood.

What had triggered this Hebrew-word approach in my mind on the plane trip? As the stewardess poured my coffee, a familiar proverb had come into my mind, "The glory of young men is their strength, and the honor of old men is their gray hair" (Proverbs 20:29). I had never thought about the implications of the proverb. But there it was in my mind so clear and succinct—the answer for the talk-show host!

What a man is depends on what season he is in. It depends on where he is on the map of manhood. It sounds like a clever answer that avoids the question, but in reality it answers the question, and does so based on very credible experience and authority. Manhood is not the same for young men as it is for older men.

I couldn't wait to get back home and look up the Hebrew words for "man" in the proverb. When I did, it confirmed what I had scribbled on a napkin at thirty thousand feet. Young men are defined by their warrior strength, old men by their wisdom. We don't expect warrior strength from old men, and it is rare we find much wisdom in young men! But both qualities are appropriate for their season. It would seem even in the issues of faith that different ages have differing spiritual challenges and demand different resources. Children need to know their sins are forgiven; younger men need to overcome their tendency to do evil; and older men need to hang in there and continue to value their spiritual persistence (1 John 2:12-14).

The Stages of the Journey

So what are the six Hebrew words that plot the course for our male journey? The first experience of maleness described is the only one we share with our feminine counterparts. The foundational Hebrew word for man is 'adam, which can refer to either male or female. As such it reflects the generic idea of all mankind, which is experienced in both males and females. For men, it says we are *creational* beings first and foremost. We are not derived from ourselves, nor do we live exclusively for ourselves, but we ultimately must reflect our Creator. As creational males we are flesh and blood, material beings — who will, however, one day return to what we really are materially — dust. Being creational means we have unique capabilities that are honorable and divine. But it also means that we are capable of using our talents for the worst of purposes and with evil devices. We must never forget who we are as men, capable of great benevolence and at the same time horrible, destructive evil.

The second word defines maleness in its most base, fundamental anatomical aspect. The Hebrew word *zakar* is the word for "male" in the phrase "God created man ['*adam*], male [*zakar*] and female" (Genesis 1:27). Hebrew lexicons list the root idea of this term as "the male protrusion, male phallus." Therefore, this word reflects the *phallic male* in his distinct sexual aspect. To describe men as phallic beings recognizes that a critical aspect of maleness is our innate sexual focus on the phallus, which either gets denied, denigrated, or perverted in our culture. We are sexual beings at our most primary (primal) level. The Bible never pretends or expects us to be otherwise. It meets us and describes us where we are, where we live and have our being. To be male is to be a phallic kind of guy, and as men we should never apologize for it, or allow it to be denigrated by women (or crass men either).

Some in the women's movement have not only neutered Christ but would call for the castration of all men in the name of rape prevention. Phallic man is the most publicized but least understood man, even by men. Some men are very phallic-aware but have sort of fixated at the phallic stage of development. On the masculine journey they stopped at Phallicville, found a sex-object, and built their whole life there. I have met men in their fifties and sixties who still think below their belts most of the time. They have never grown up and moved on in their maleness. They have never learned that sexual energy must be channeled constructively.

The next stop on the journey is that of the much-publicized experience of the *warrior*. From Robert Bly to Sam Keen, there exists much concern for the lack of true warriors in our society. The Hebrew word *gibbor* reflects this male in his warring strength. Young adult men war on the athletic fields, war in their minds in graduate schools, war in business, war in Southeast and Southwest Asia. They war to be the best, the biggest, the toughest, the richest, the smartest, the most published and well-known. They kill the competition, opposing viewpoints, their declared enemies, and sometimes their own marriages and families.

This competitive warring is also a part of being a man. But the warrior, likewise, has been devalued in our society. The warrior is a killer—violent, unthinking, uncaring, and abusing—say many women and men influenced by women. But a nation without its warriors is in a precarious posture, as the Kuwaitis now know. The important question is not whether warriors are important, but whether, when they fight and go to war, they are fighting for the right things. Strength, combat, and competition are masculine traits, and unless they are rediscovered and valued by both the men and women in our society we are in serious trouble.

The warrior is often over-glorified. He is the honored hero. However, there is a reality to warfare that often gets overlooked. No military recruiter in his right mind (in peace-time) reveals that in raising one's right hand and being sworn to obey the orders of his commanding officers and Commander in Chief, the implication exists that he could get killed or wounded. That doesn't sell well anymore. Even during World War II, I can't remember any posters saying, "Uncle Sam Wants You . . . To Die for Him." But the reality of any combat is clear. Warriors get wounded. Some die young.

The fourth Hebrew word for man is the word *enosh*. This word describes man in his weakness, in his frailty, and in his woundedness . . . the *wounded warrior* . . . the *wounded male*. Much is being written today about the wounded male. He has been wounded by abusive and absent fathers; by domineering mothers and teachers; by the educational system; by toxic takeovers in business; by layoffs; by failure, by success; by alcohol; by divorce; by his own friendlessness; by poverty, by wealth. No matter what brought the sword to his heart, the warrior is now wounded and bleeding. He is in need and often doesn't know it.

The wounded male has been called the metaphor for the nineties. I have been in nursing homes and have met wounded men in their eighties. They didn't get the promotion they wanted and it wounded them for life. They never recovered. They got lost in a huge black hole on the masculine

journey . . . the black hole called woundedness. We as men can
stay wounded for the rest of our lives very easily. Woundedness is a part of the male experience—a very important part. It
is not abnormal, but a predictable experience on the male journey and one for which very few men are prepared. But it is sur-
vivable and can lead to another refreshing male experience.

The most common American male image of manhood is
probably the solitary man on horseback, who knows exactly
what he is all about and who has said no to many other voices
in his life. In the movie *City Slickers*, Jack Palance plays the
aged, weatherworn mentor for the younger "city slickers" (lead
played by Billy Crystal). He is qualified to be a mentor because
he has sorted out the important from the unimportant and has
become the solitary male who no longer listens to the outside
influences of culture and women. (The only women he loved
he rode away from!)

The fifth Hebrew term reflects this differentiated male ruling over his own spirit. The word *'ish* reflects man as the *ruler*
of his own soul, being independent of outside considerations.
This is the differentiated man—one who is his own man, who
knows who he really is and what he is all about, apart from
anyone else. The ruling male is thus attributal, in that he is
usually characterized by his own attributes. But unlike Jack
Palance in *City Slickers*, the *'ish* kind of man is *not alone*.

The ruling man is also seen in his relationships and in fact
is known by them. This term best describes his relationships,
especially with women. The implication is clear. A man cannot
become the ruler of his own soul and genuine in his relationships until he has been through some wounding. It is only
the wounded male who can begin to rule with more wisdom
and not be attracted to every voice asking him to do something. The phallic male and the warrior are very susceptible to
error in this regard. But through wounding a man takes on a
learned perspective of life. He is not as attracted to or tempted
by everything that comes down the pike. He can begin to listen to the voice of God more clearly, and to the leanings of
his own conscience and values. He can direct his paths more

purposefully because of his clearer vision of life and living in accordance with biblical truth. He is no longer afraid to be a maverick, to go against the grain, to do what he wants to do or what he really thinks God wants him to do. It is a time for serious integration and dedication to his core values. This is an important part of the male experience. Some men do it, many don't. For those who don't, life stagnates and their souls may die. They stay wounded or numb for the rest of their lives. For the man who starts to rule his own soul, life gets more exciting and leads to his greatest contributions and achievements.

While becoming differentiated and individualized has become the goal of much psychotherapy, I feel there is an inherent temptation when "being an individual" is the primary goal. To become the ruler of one's own soul can also very easily turn to a certain self-absorption and living life totally as an individual. I know retired pastors who live in total isolation. I know executives and military officers who are ROTJ (retired on the job!). Though this is not the thrust of the word *ish*, I have seen men seriously embrace what they wanted out of life, and then go out and do it. They played golf every day, got away from everyone and everything that caused them pain, and just tried to be the self-actualized person they had become for the rest of their lives. The biblical male journey, however, does not end this way.

The last meaningful stop on our journey is at the Hebrew word for elder. This word, *zaken*, is the word that was used in the proverb that came to my mind on the plane that day. The word means, literally, "gray-headed," but the usage normally reflects the idea of the wise mentor or *sage*. The gray-headed male is not the confused, solitary senior-citizen male often portrayed in movies and prime time. The biblical image sees this man connected to all of life and making his finest and most important contribution to the community and culture. He is the one who sits at the political, civic, and religious centers of the society making his most significant contribution. He is also a mentor as he sits at the gates of the cities imparting the wisdom of the ages to the younger men. In most ancient societies he was the man among men, the man to whom the younger men looked for mentoring, guidance, nurture, and understanding of life. He was also the one who granted to younger men the honor of being accepted fully into the adult male community. To sit in the circle of the sages was indeed the lifelong pursuit of young men.

Today, the image of the elderly male has been changed to one who sits in retirement homes, separated from the younger men, watching television all day and waiting to die. Our sages today have either been scorned into hiding or they don't exist. It's time we find them and put them to work, or start giving the younger men a vision for being sages. The gray hair is not something to be covered with Grecian Formula, but something to be honored by all men. It's part of the male journey; in fact, it is *the* destination and completion of the trip. Let's celebrate it.

That's where we are headed in this book. I hope it will provide direction for you as a man, and for women as well — women who want to understand what men struggle with. But understand, I'll be addressing the man primarily.

These stages are not intended to be necessarily a chronological prediction. As men we live at many points on the map at the same time. In this sense the stopping places are more logical than chronological. On the other hand, there does seem to be a certain implied order in the development of these words. It's harder to be a sage without the experience of being a warrior and being wounded. Wisdom always flows from life experience, and unfortunately, that life experience is often negative. It is difficult trying to wage war with wisdom without the experience of having been wounded.

As I write these words from my late midlife perspective, I am very much aware that I am still creational. But the body reveals the fact that I am aging. From the color of my hair to the new holes in my belt to the aches I feel after mowing the lawn, I am very creational. I always will be. I am also very phallic. I have a beautiful wife, but I always feel the psychosexual tug from commercials selling far more than soap. The phallus does not go away with age, use, or disuse. I am still very phallic. On some of my good days, I still see myself as the warrior. I still dream the impossible dreams, want to build some glorious institution that will carry on my name, or write a best seller (maybe this book!). But I have been wounded — by churches, by institutions, by trusted friends, by broken promises, by things not turning out the way I thought they should or would. On some days my wounding incapacitates me. I hope that out of my pain I have gained some wisdom about what not to do, or what never to attempt again. I think I'm learning to rule my own soul better. I'm learning to say no more often, to realize that the world or the organization or this day does not really depend totally on me. I don't think I'm a sage yet, but I want to be. I want my best years to be ahead of me, not behind me. I want to make a contribution in the lives of others, both male and female. I want to feel connected to more of life than I am right now. I don't want to end life in a retirement home watching reruns and counting minutes till the next mealtime. There seem to be so many more important things to give back to life when you have the most to give. I hope I remember to think this way when I am eighty!

That summarizes the course of the book and the stages of manhood I am attempting to define. For the past year I have been "test-marketing" this material in men's seminars and retreats around the country. What started out as a few Hebrew words scrawled on a napkin has now grown to an entire weekend seminar that I put on for men. The masculine journey approach seems to provide these men with a useful frame in which they can understand themselves and their experiences. I usually conclude my presentation by asking men to share where they are on the journey. This is the most rewarding time of the weekend. At this point, I see how the various stages have given these men a handle on understanding their feelings. Common statements include: "I am still very much the warrior," or "I didn't realize that being wounded is an important aspect of maleness," or "I've never admitted before how much my phallic maleness still influences my life, even as a Christian." These responses have shown me that I was on target with these ancient Hebrew terms. Or rather, that God was on target in providing a language so descriptive of the entire masculine adventure.

I want to make clear that there exists much room for variety and creativity along this road. Our God is a God of variety, and since we are made in His image, there are probably an infinite number of ways one can proceed along this road. These pages simply record the experiences that seem to be common among both the biblical and contemporary images of manhood. In that commonality there exists a rich amount of variety.

I'll conclude this introduction by quoting from the excellent book of essays on manhood edited by Keith Thompson. He writes, "Masculinity does appear to be embedded in — and to be the expression of — certain elementary, rudimentary, 'deep structures.' Even so, these pathways clearly provide for a remarkable degree of variety, diversity and 'natural drift' in masculine expression in cultures throughout the world."[11] Hopefully, this book illustrates one of the ways of understanding some of these deep structures or common ways of viewing the male experience that will answer the question "What *is* a man?"

Creational Male — 'Adam: The Noble Savage

◆

Man with all his noble qualities
still bears in his bodily frame
the indelible stamp of his lowly origin.

CHARLES ROBERT DARWIN
The Descent of Man

Do Impulses toward sadistic cruelty
lurk in the depths of every human psyche?

ANTHONY STORR
Human Destructiveness

BY COMMON HIGH school categories I was a jock. I played football, basketball, and baseball. My stomach was flat, my thighs strong, and my neck a muscular eighteen inches. Today, I'm flabby and weak with a puffy neck. But I still see myself as that in-shape eighteen-year-old who can go out and play one-on-one for several hours and get up the next morning without a pain or ache. The ambitions and desires of youth are still with me and very much a part of my self-estimate. But time, age, and a lifestyle that no longer includes daily rigorous practice schedules have caught up with me. I'm not what I used to be. I have had to realize I am a very mortal being. The realization of such makes us confront much about our own humanity.

Spiritually, the same tension exists. Some days I see myself in heavenly terms, preaching great sermons, living righteously so others may wish to emulate me. Then reality hits. Whether it's an argument with my wife, or problems with my employer, or just wondering where the money is going to come from for bills, tuition, and food, I see very quickly that I am no saint. Within every upward desire, there is a countering downward pull. As men, no matter how old we may be, there exists a certain nobility about us, but within the most noble of desires there also exists an often surprising savagery. To cite Margaret Mead's often-used term for the uncivilized people groups she studied, we as men (and all humankind) are *noble savages*.

As noted in the previous chapter, the first stage on this masculine journey is the only one that includes our feminine counterparts as well. God made *both* sexes in His own image. The term the biblical writers used to describe this image is the Hebrew word *'adam.*[1] God said, "Let Us make man [*'adam*] in Our image. . . . And God created man [*'adam*] in His own image, in the image of God He created him; *male and female* He created them" (Genesis 1:26-27, emphasis added). So everything that is true of creational male is also true of creational female. We share the creaturely components expressed in this word with our sisters. This says, at the outset, that both male and female share much in terms of needs, capabilities, and responsibilities. However, the other five words will focus on how men experience their humanness in contrast to women on the different points on the masculine journey. So what does it mean to be creational, whether male or female?

What Does *'Adam* Mean?

The Hebrew word *'adam* provides a vivid portrait of what the essence of human experience is. Ancient Near-Eastern usage of the word includes the ideas of "dark, red soil and red blood."[2] Therefore, the word depicts mankind at the most base level of flesh, blood, and dirt. It suggests what we really are as humans and men. The usage of *'adam* reveals four ideas about what it means to be a creational kind of guy.

Created for Relationships

To be a creational male means to realize we as men have not been created for ourselves. The prophet Jeremiah declared that *'adam* was not created for himself and therefore should be very fearful about trusting in himself (Jeremiah 10:23, 17:5). Moses made it very clear that "man does not live by bread alone" (Deuteronomy 8:3). We are made in God's image and, as such, we are made to have a relationship with our Creator. This strikes very deep at the heart of male independence, especially the rank independence from God we see in many men. But to be creational means that we as men owe something back to God. We are not created and given life in order to go our merry way without even saying so much as "thank you."

Inherent in the concept of being made in "God's image" is that we are His representatives on earth. In one sense, we show forth to the world and perhaps angels what God is like. In ancient cultures, images were personal portraits of the kings that allowed the citizens to know what their ruler looked like (see Daniel 3:2). If this is true, then the King of creation has made us humans to rule as His vice-regents on earth and show forth what His rule should look like on earth. It is awesome to think that God is looking to me to reveal what He is like, but that seems to be the intended meaning of the term *image of God.*

Having a relationship with the living God also means that in this ruling function we as men must form a certain benevolent relationship with the earth and our fellowmen. Our joint rulership (men and women) of the earth suggests not the progressive environmental rape that we have seen by the "Christian" industrial nations. The rulership envisioned in Genesis 1:28 implies the rule of wisdom, care, and stewardship of God's territory. When the law was given, respect for property, boundaries, and natural resources was given with as much authority as was the Ten Commandments (Deuteronomy 5:6-21, 20:19-20, 22:1-4, 25:4; Proverbs 22:28). In modern terms, as trite as it might seem, this means that it is manly to recycle and have genuine concern for the welfare of our planet.

I don't want my grandkids to live in the trash heap that our lovely earth could become if we merely do nothing.

This accountability is also extended to those living on the earth. The question from the early chapters of Genesis still echoes down through the hallways of history. Cain, in feigned innocence, asked the Lord, "Am I my brother's keeper?" (Genesis 4:9). The answer is obvious . . . for all times. Yes!!! I am my brother's keeper. I am held accountable for how I treat my fellow man. It is upon 'adam that the issues of justice and kindness are placed along with humility before God. This is what the Lord requires of all creational men:

> He has told you, O man ['adam], what is good;
> And what does the LORD require of you
> But to do justice, to love kindness,
> And to walk humbly with your God? (Micah 6:8)

The Israelite was held accountable for how he treated his fellow countrymen and even the passersby (Deuteronomy 22:1-4, 14:29). The New Testament picks up this theme and imputes the same responsibility to the believer, even toward those outside the Church (Matthew 5:44, Romans 12:14-20, Galatians 6:10).

As men we can try to run away from our Creator and our divinely given responsibilities, but we must realize that we are running away from not only ourselves but also from what it means to be manly. I have known men who were unconsciously running from God for years. Thinking Christianity was for women or wimpy men, or seeing no relevance in what goes on in most churches, they made their choice to pursue other passions. I personally don't blame them. I think it speaks highly of them. As Elton Trueblood has observed,

> The "sacred fellowship" may be so taken up with struggles for institutional prestige and personal power that the honest seeker is disgusted. There is no denying that many of the best people are outside the churches

precisely because they *are* the best people. The fact that they have been disgusted is something in their favor; at least it shows that their standards are encouragingly high.[3]

But when these very men finally understand Christianity as a personal relationship with Christ and see the masculinity of Christ, they respond differently. I believe all men are "Christ haunted" and hunted down until they truly see what it is they are rejecting. I have worked with many men who—when they finally see they have been running away from a caricature of Christianity and toward religious activity, therapy, infidelity, and compulsive work—fall down with tears in their eyes and see the One for whom they were made. The Bible calls this repentance; we may also call it being manly!

Without accepting the creaturely realities of being made by and for our heavenly Father, we cannot be the men we should be. This is the beginning point, the first stop on the male journey. Without beginning here we won't develop any further. Without this relationship, we won't grow up as men and become the men we were made to be.

'Adam also reveals man in his relations with women. Man is created "male and female." To be a creational male also means to be created for the feminine counterpart. In the biblical development, the feminine is seen as providing the relational aspect so desperately needed in the male but not provided by the animal kingdom (see Genesis 2:18-25).[4] The woman illustrates, in her relation to the male, a mirror image of 'adam, but of a different sort. In the woman 'adam sees himself, one human to another but utterly different from the other animals. When he gazes on this freshly created woman, he quickly notices the differences with celebration joy. "This one (the woman) I will take!"

In doing premarital counseling, I'm always fascinated to see how God brings two people together who are so opposite of each other (the present writer and his wife not excluded!). Over the years I have become convinced this is more than just the usual explanation that "opposites attract." There is something far deeper here . . . something creational. God created the sexes as opposites whereby in each other there would be a mystical and magical quality to the relationship. God grounds the marital relationship in the mysterious concept of diversity living together in unity. Unless this is understood as true intimacy, the tendency is to see the differences, over time, as only grounds for "incompatibility" and ultimately divorce.

To be creational means we are created for relationships not only with our Creator but also with our counterpart. As men, when we look into the mirror after showering and see our unique sexual equipment, it is a reminder that we are made for another — another of a different sort. We were made by God to express the creativity and plurality of what it means to be a creational male in relationship.

Created with Dignity

I read as much as I can in the general counseling field in order to facilitate my own growth and understanding. Go into any shopping mall bookstore and browse through the self-help section and you will see multitudinous titles on how to improve one's self-image or recover lost self-esteem. General audience books always amaze me, because the authors rarely reveal the source from which they have derived their assumptions. It seems the entire self-help movement has assumed as its first premise that self-esteem is something to be valued, sought, and recovered. Now, I don't debate the premise as a Christian writer, I just wonder how writers who have no theological or philosophical orientation (or so they often claim) can assume such a massive first premise. *Why* should the self be valued and improved?

As I understand modern psychological literature, there is very little explanation as to why this first assumption exists. Again, I don't debate it, even though at times I think they have overdone it; I only wonder how they get what they get. For me, the only way to understand the concept of self-esteem as something to be valued is to ground it in the "image of God."

In other words, it is a value because it is created, and if created then it has worth and significance. If God has made both male and female in His own image, there is then something to be valued and esteemed in the self of every human being. If we are mere accidents from some primordial ooze that somehow got here, then it is hard for me to see how there is much to be valued or esteemed. Perhaps we are seeing in our violent society today the long-term implications of many decades of this teaching. If humans have no special creational worth, then why not blow other humans away, or treat them inhumanly?

To be creaturely means to have a dignity and worth not derived from our performance or obtainments but by our birth and being. As men, we have value because we merely *are*, not because of what we do or accomplish. I can lose my job, my marriage, my kids, and suffer the loss of self-esteem, but this does not mean I have none. I know few men who have this reality so deeply rooted in their psyches that they never suffer from the performance syndrome. But at least it is encouraging to know I have value for no other reason than just being. I am a man, created by a God who loves me and who made me in His own image and as a unique individual unlike any other human being on earth. This is the apparent reason God gives any thought to mankind. The psalmist says, "What is man . . . and the son of man ['*adam*], that Thou dost care for him?" (Psalm 8:4). It is only to man ('*adam*) that God has given His own spirit (Genesis 6:3) and the very breath of life (2:7).

When I have been disgraced by events or circumstances, I fight to regain some sense of dignity. This struggle for dignity (often wrongly referred to as pride) reveals only who and what I really am—a creational male. God put into the legislation of Israel many laws and statutes that were designed to protect the life and reputation of her citizens (Exodus 20:16, 23:1; Deuteronomy 17:6). In my fight for self-affirmation, I am revealing the basic fabric of what I am and how I am made. The work of psychologists and self-help writers only affirms this reality, whether they realize it or not. The therapeutic remedies that are designed to recover or develop self-esteem, and the self-help literature, only affirm this intrinsic, deeply rooted but unexplained value. The value of human dignity, and thus self-esteem, is only explainable by creation and a Creator!

Creational Mortality

The original dignity with which God made man did not last long. Apparently, had 'adam not sinned, he could have continued to eat at the tree of life and been immortal (Genesis 2:17, 3:22-24). But being cast out of the garden, he lost his access to the tree of life and its life-giving properties. Thus, a death sentence was placed on mankind, and the nobility of the creational-earthly vice-regent was faced with an ever-growing mortality. The reality men often deny or pretend doesn't affect them is this sense of mortality. We think we will live forever; we won't have heart attacks, lose our capabilities, our health, or our minds. But sooner or later the wages of our own mortality encroach more and more upon our lives. Eventually, we must face the startling revelation that life must be lived within the limits of breath and death. The duration of our lives is not determined by us. We do not have the ability to govern our own destiny.

Despite all the motivational speakers and self-help pop psychology that tells us we can do anything we set our minds on, the stark, naked reality exists that we are very dependent beings. I cannot guarantee for myself or anyone else that I will be alive tomorrow. My very breath is in my Creator's hands (Ecclesiastes 12:6-7), and I must go to sleep at night trusting Him to keep me breathing during my sleep. The psalmist also says the very sleep is His gift (Psalm 127:2)!

The psalmist also uses the word 'adam to describe the reality of this mortality. He says even though 'adam may try to "buy" his way out of his own mortality, it is an impossibility. He reveals,

No man ['adam] can by any means redeem his brother,
Or give to God a ransom for him —
For the redemption of his soul is costly,

And he should cease trying forever—
That he should live on eternally;
That he should not undergo decay. (Psalm 49:7-9)

No one escapes the decay of men. Eventually, we as men must face the fact we will die the death of all men and suffer the fate of all mankind (Numbers 16:29). This is the tombstone theology that is rarely taught in either seminaries or churches. Given enough time we are being gradually turned back to what we essentially are—dust (Psalm 90:3). But the cosmetics, health, and exercise industries would like us to think otherwise. I believe in exercise, though I don't do as much as I should, and I believe in painting the barn when it needs it. But the youth-oriented fashion and movie industries would try to make us believe we can cover up or conceal the fact that even the superstars will develop wrinkles and sagging bodies.

Gail Sheehy in a recent book, *The Silent Passage*, tells how the word *menopause* cannot even be uttered around Hollywood. She comments that going to Hollywood to talk about menopause was like going to Las Vegas to sell savings accounts.[5] Where youthful sexuality and the emphasis on appearance that goes with it are worshiped, there is rampant denial of mortality and its implications. But no matter how wealthy, healthy, intelligent, or beautiful we are, mortality ultimately strikes all of us. We cannot buy our way out of or around the final reality that we will age, decline, and face the deterioration of our minds, bodies, and spirits. We may put it off for a while with cosmetics, exercise, and the surgeon's knife, but eventually the principle of the universe—decay—wins. We are mortal.

The psalmist continues,

For He sees that even wise men die;
The stupid and the senseless alike perish,
And leave their wealth to others.
Their inner thought is, that their houses are forever,

And their dwelling places to all generations;
They have called their lands after their own names.
But man in his pomp will not endure.
(Psalm 49:10-12)

Fleeting mortality became one of the main conclusions Solomon arrived at about the lives of the rich and famous. In this regard, he is an ancient Robin Leach. Solomon had both the time and the money to devote himself to the serious contemplation of everything that claimed to amount to something. It would be like watching television advertising all day long and then going out to see if the claims could be proved. Does driving a Pontiac really grant excitement, or wearing Guess jeans impart a certain animal magnetism for a man? He asks, "For what does a man ['adam] get in all his labor and in his striving with which he labors under the sun?" His answer? "All his days his task is painful and grievous; even at night his mind does not rest. This too is vanity" (Ecclesiastes 2:22-23). Solomon's conclusion is this: *All claims fail.* Fundamentally, life always promises more than it can deliver, and the result is a sense of mortal uneasiness and emptiness.

This is a reality men in my experience do not like to face. It usually takes the loss of job, marriage, or health to finally make this reality a part of our personal conscience and convictions. Facing the mortality of life and finally figuring out that life is beyond our comprehension is not easy for men (or women). But it is a necessary part of the male map. It is an experience that must be embraced as an important aspect of being a creational male. To talk of mortality leads logically and naturally to the more shadowy side of our nobility. For you see, we are noble savages!

Creational Savagery

When Margaret Mead first started studying the primitive peoples of Polynesia and Micronesia, what she encountered was not the expected savagery that was often portrayed by

Western writers and missionaries. Instead, she found family systems where parents cared for their young and societies that were organized with systems of justice and fairness, though these differed from Western conceptions. Impressed by the noble aspirations of these "savages," she consequently coined the term *noble savage*. She was impressed by the unexpected and unexplainable nobility found among the most primitive of peoples. Today, there is a striking similarity going on in reverse. Amid all the emphasis on high aspirations in "civilized" countries, the real question is how to explain the surprising amount and extent of violence, greed, and human degradation. When we begin to look underneath the veneer of this noble culture, what we find is not the expected beauty and purity of individual benevolence, but a sheer confrontation with evil. The person in the appearance of a saint is a savage! How can this be explained?

The Scriptures simply explain this condition in terms of the Fall. The earthly vice-regent of God has had his crown stolen and has fallen prey to his own earthly rule. He is now ruled by his own passions, ambitions, compulsions, and addictions, rather than ruling in the divine majesty for which he was created. Made in the image of God, he still longs and yearns for such, and apart from divine grace extended through Jesus Christ remains a slave to them throughout his life. Even when the resources of grace are applied to his life in Christ, the struggle with the savage remains. The flesh still rages against the movement of the Spirit within even the renewed male and female (Galatians 5:16-17).

The savagery of the soul should not surprise us as men. Though we are made in God's image and are creational—that is, possessing great capabilities for good—we are also free to pursue unholy courses and to become the most evil of men. As men, we must embrace both aspects in ourselves. Without embracing both, we are set up to become the most abhorrent of men. Our tendency is to not accept this picture as a true reality. We all carry airbrushed portraits of ourselves that show no blemishes or scars. But historical realities such

as the Holocaust stand as stark reminders of who we really are
as humans.

In an attempt to understand the psychology of human
destruction, a British psychiatrist writes,

> The concentration camps required large numbers of
> guards of both sexes. It did not make sense to suppose
> that all these people were sociopaths or sadists. One
> had to accept that quite ordinary citizens of what had
> been one of the most cultured nations on earth could
> be persuaded, without too much difficulty and on an
> unprecedented scale, to treat their fellow citizens with
> barbarous cruelty.[6]

One of my Jewish friends puts it even more graphically. Upon
visiting one of the extermination camps, he noted that in the
middle of the camp was the commandant's quarters. One went
through a stone fence with a white picket door. Inside was a
grassy lawn complete with a set of swings. My friend at that
point uttered, "My God, this man had his children here." At
the entrance to the house, beside the door on a coatrack, were
his Nazi overcoat and hat. In the living room was a piano, with
music of Bach, Beethoven, and Handel. His next thought was,
"This man gassed Jews all day long, had them buried in lime
and covered over, then came home, took off his Nazi uniform,
played with his kids, and sang Christmas carols!"

What kind of man can do this? *The kind of man I am.* I have
done the same kind of "compartmentalizing" in my mind in
order to carry out someone else's unjust wishes on many occasions. The only difference is the degree and the job description.
The psychology is the same.

Until I realize the evil that I am capable of, I don't really
believe that Jesus Christ means all that much. I may know I
am saved, but I have no real idea of what I am saved from.
I believe I am just now beginning to have a glimpse of this
reality after twenty-five years of being a Christian. Only now
am I seeing how utterly incapable of righteousness I am.

This realization should not surprise me, for the Scriptures clearly teach it.

Early in the biblical development, God uttered His conclusions about mankind ('adam): "Then the LORD saw that the wickedness of man was great on the earth, and that every intent of the thoughts of his heart was only evil continually" (Genesis 6:5). Again, He says, "For the intent of man's ['adam] heart is evil from his youth" (8:21). This is the reason humans cannot see God while in the flesh. Moses wanted to see God so that he could have the assurance of His presence, but God reminded him, "You cannot see My face, for no man ['adam] can see Me and live" (Exodus 33:20). The writer of Ecclesiastes takes evil further. He writes, "Furthermore, the hearts of the sons of men ['adam] are full of evil, and insanity is in their hearts throughout their lives" (9:3). He adds that because of the lack of human justice, men are given to become violent and do evil to each other (8:11). This sheds much light on our inner city violence and such things as the Rodney King beating, trial, final verdict, and the resultant Los Angeles riots.

As men, we can very easily fall into the naive position that there are good ol' boys (good guys) and wicked men. In other words, we have divided the world into two groups of people, good and bad. We, of course, are the good guys. But this is both psychological lunacy and theological madness. Remember Ecclesiastes? We have *insanity* in our hearts.

As Alexander Solzhenitsyn reminded the West from his Gulag cell, "The line that divides good and evil is not a line that divides good men from bad men, but a line which cuts through the middle of every human heart."[7] How else can we explain the Herods, Neros, Caligulas, Hitlers, Khomeinis, Noriegas, and Saddam Husseins? How else can I explain the inner Hitler-like impulses that I feel when I don't get my way, or when someone else gets in my way, or when I want to get rid of someone who is so unlike me that I can't tolerate him anymore? When I am tempted to use intimidation, force, manipulation, and lying, how do I explain that within myself? The answer is that my inner creational royalty has fallen prey to the savage within. When I am treated like the savage that I am, the royal spirit cries out within me like the elephant man saying, "I am a man; I am a human being." That's what we as men are—noble savages. All of us, regardless of our race, color, or creed—we all have this fight within. None of my evil responses should ever surprise me, because both aspects of my nature are true at the same time. I am created as a royal son to rule my Father's Kingdom, but I have fallen and become a savage. This is the first stop on the masculine journey. We must embrace both aspects in ourselves to genuinely encounter what maleness in its fullness means.

The Noble Savage: Solomon

In each of these chapters I will try give a biblical portrait or type of male experience that characterizes what the contents of the chapter have been talking about. When I think of the noble savage or creational male, my mind is immediately drawn to Solomon. Solomon, as the Davidic king, is seen in both the royal aspect of creational greatness and his extreme fallenness. When God offers to grant him anything that he requests, Solomon asks for wisdom. In response, God says, "Because you have asked this thing and have not asked for yourself long life, nor have asked riches for yourself, nor have you asked for the life of your enemies, . . . I have also given you what you have not asked, both riches and honor, so that there will not be any among the kings like you all your days" (1 Kings 3:11,13).

Solomon uses his wisdom and wealth to build the first temple in Jerusalem. It was into this temple that the very presence of God entered (2 Chronicles 7:1). He collected the wisdom of the ancients, and dignitaries came from all over the known world to learn of Solomon's riches and wisdom (2 Chronicles 9:1-12, Proverbs 25:1). His wealth, worth, glory, and accomplishments reflect the 'adam kind of man at his highest—creational, serving, caring, generating for good. He knew he stood in the place of God, being responsible for God's concerns in the world even to the lowliest of his servants. But Solomon was also a student of the aspirations and expectations of life. To this end he devoted himself as only one of the greatest of tenth-century kings could (Ecclesiastes 2:4-9).[8]

The more Solomon pursued the pleasures and satisfactions of life, the more he came to the conclusion of man's mortality, and that man's ultimate destiny was futility. Hence, the royal man embraces mortal aspects of his being. But the commentary on Solomon does not end here. The further one reads in the historical account, the more one encounters a story of a fallen prince, a king who, by his own admission, ends up serving his pleasures and passions. Solomon numbers his palace-pleasure entourage in the thousands, including both men and women (Ecclesiastes 2:8, 7:28). He built a house for God, but he built an even bigger house for himself.[9] He loved foreign women and had over seven hundred wives, many of whom turned his heart away from the Lord (1 Kings 11:1-13). Solomon had no problem in raising a first-class army and multiplied his defensive capabilities throughout Israel. To do this he used foreign legions and forced labor from those he defeated. This was in direct opposition to the credo of godly kings to not multiply horses, wives, or wealth (Deuteronomy 17:16-17).

In other words, Solomon was not only the royal, noble, spiritually minded monarch, but also a man of lower-nature debauchery. He loved his women, his wealth, and the power his reign brought him. Solomon was a sinner. His abilities were used for good and evil. The legacy he left was a symbol of his divided heart. His two sons, after his death, split the one kingdom in two, which remained divided throughout the rest of Israel's history. Solomon is the noble savage, the creational male, the first man we as men must realize we are. His modern counterparts are inside traders and shylock televangelists, anyone rich in ability and potentiality who ends up using it for selfish pleasure and personal gain.

This first stop is a confrontation with our inherent nobility and savagery. We must never lose sight of either and be the men we ought to be. But sooner or later, we will begin to realize that our approach to life is radically different from that of our girlfriends, wives, and female associates. After all, the details of our *masculine* journey differ from the feminine experience. The differences begin at birth (and before in the womb) when the doctor says, "It's a boy."

CHAPTER THREE

The Phallic Male—
Zakar: The Mysterious
Taskmaster

◆

The passions should be held in reverence.
EDGAR ALLEN POE
"The Raven"

The loins are the place of judgment.
N. O. BROWN
Quoted in *Fire in the Belly* by Sam Keen

ONCE CONFINED TO the father's waiting room in hospitals, a man now has the opportunity to be a significant player in the birth of his children. The decade in which my children were born illustrated this massive social change. When Charis, my firstborn daughter, arrived, I was with my mother-in-law in the smoke-filled waiting room. Anxiously observing every doctor and nurse who entered the room, we sat there awaiting the big announcement. The waiting room was my place then. When Ashley, my second-born, arrived, I was allowed into the delivery room *immediately following* the birth to photograph the proud new mother with child. It was a special moment. But by the time my wife, Cinny, was pregnant with Graham, number three, times had changed significantly. Now I could be the coach. I could be in the delivery room and actually be a real player in the event. After I held my wife's hand and helped

47

her with her breathing, the doctor caught the little person who emerged from inside her. The doctor held the baby up and declared, "It's a boy." He then allowed me to cut the cord!

Years later, I now wonder, "How did the doctor know that?" How did he know my son was male rather than female? When I tell this story at men's conferences and retreats, everyone laughs. But it is no laughing matter. The doctor made his determination the way every doctor, midwife, or father has made the determination in every society since the beginning of time. It has been only in the last couple of decades that we have become confused about it. In the past, one checked out the genitals and made the announcement. That was that! But today, things are not so easy. It seems maleness and femaleness have become something to be debated and politicized. This is where the ancient wisdom of the Scriptures provides some additional help in acting as a map for our masculine experience.

The Phallus as the Organ of Gender Discrimination

The second word used for man or male is the Hebrew word *zakar*, which is usually translated as "male" in opposition to woman.[1] This word is used eighty-two times in the Old Testament, but when the Semitic roots for the word are examined, the primary verbal idea is "to be sharp, or pointed."[2] Now, the connotation is not that of being a "sharp" dresser or such. The meaning has to do with the male protrusion, hence the male penis or phallus. When Arabic (also a Semitic language using the same three consonantal bases for words) is consulted, the word for male (*dakar*) and the word for penis is the same word.[3] In other words, the Scriptures root male identity and sexuality firmly in anatomy, rather than in psychology or sociology. Male identity, as determined by modern psychology, says, "You are a male if you feel like one." Sociology might say, "You are male if you do the kinds of things that the given culture says you should do to be considered male." Obviously, in this rapidly changing culture mixed with the garden variety of pop psychologies, male identity can mean virtually anything.

The Bible simply defines manhood by the phallus, the very way the doctor did when my son was born. *I am a male, whether I feel like it or not, or whether I ever do anything considered masculine by the culture in which I am living.* This is the fixed point on the male journey that roots my identity as a man in something that will never change. Yes, sex-change operations take place, but they only illustrate the complete rebellion and perversion of the concept. The entirety of the Scriptures reflect the simple twofold division of the entire human and animal kingdom into male (*zakar*) and female (*neqevah*). The female term likewise has anatomical overtones in meaning, namely having the ideas of being "bored through, and pierced."[4] This roots the essential identity of both sexes in the equipment they show up with at birth. Such equipment we know has been developing differently from the time of conception.

On the day my son, Graham, was born, he did not know what it meant to be phallic. This awareness, with all its associated ideas and problems, came later with puberty. But for now let me continue to address how the Scriptures use this word *zakar*.

The Phallus as Determiner of Religious Service
The feminist era has made all gender differentiation into political discrimination. Therefore, when some feminists read the Bible all they see is the sexual discrimination that they believe dominated the biblical writers' instruction. However, the Bible says only what it says, and often what we see in it is what we want to see. It is very easy to view the Bible through the cultural or political glasses that we have already embraced as correct. Therefore, we go to the Bible to justify our own political or theological correctness. And we make our modern agendas lord, rather than going to the Bible and seeking to understand its message in a radically different time and place. There are many things in the Bible that seem unfair or unjust to contemporary readers, but the reason they seem unfair is because modern standards of fairness differ radically from what we read in the Bible. The real question I need to ask myself as

a biblical reader is, "Where did I get my current standards for fairness?" We get them through the agency of our modern cultural perspectives and influences. Therefore, the fact that spiritual service in the Old Testament was regulated by gender seems offensive to modern readers. I can't answer why this is so or what it really means to the church today, but I do know there are differences. So what are the differences?

First, the celebrative animal offerings made during Israel's feasts were made on the basis of gender. Heads of households on Passover were to bring a male lamb (Exodus 12:5). For a guilt offering only a female sheep or goat was allowed (Leviticus 5:6). Peace offerings could be either male or female (3:1,6), while all freewill offerings had to be male (22:19). Why? I have no idea! No reason is given in the text for the differences. But what it does reveal is that each individual was required to worship God in specific ways. I don't believe there was any preference toward maleness or femaleness in this system. However, some feminists have noted that only the male was required to bring a sacrifice (Exodus 23:17, 34:23; Deuteronomy 16:16). This is true. It was also true that only males were counted in the national census (Numbers 1:2,20,22), and only males could be priests (Exodus 28:1, Leviticus 8:1-3). Furthermore, only males could be killed in mass murder and used as cannon fodder in war, while the women and children were often allowed to live (Deuteronomy 20:13-14).[5] Men also got to pay far more money than women for making the same vows (Leviticus 27:3,5-6).

These differences seem just as unfair to me as a man when I view them through the lens of my modern "enlightened" society. Why should I as a man have to pay more money than a woman for making the same religious vow? Or why should I have to risk my own life in warfare, when at least women have the option of being servants of the winning army and staying alive? These stipulations do not seem fair. One can view these differences as one would examine the bark of trees while missing what is going on in the forest. Even though I don't know exactly why these differences exist—since no explanation is given—it is my generalization that what it says about the phallic male is that there is *no conflict between sexuality and spirituality*. We are called and addressed by God in terminology that describes who and what we are—*zakar*, phallic males.

Possessing a penis places unique requirements upon men before God in how they are to worship Him. We are called to worship God as phallic kinds of guys, not as some sort of androgynous, neutered nonmales, or the feminized males so popular in many feminist-enlightened churches. We are told by God to worship Him in accordance with what we are, phallic men.

The Phallus as the Symbol of Dedication and Connection
Years ago we moved our family to the beautiful isle of Hawaii. Like all newcomers we toured the outer islands and took in the ancient Hawaiian sites and visited the museums of Hawaiian culture. On one occasion I remember staring at various ancient Hawaiian artifacts. As my wife noticed the same statue I was looking at, she questioned, "Why is it so large?" Her question was not related to the overall size of the statue but the size of its protruding phallus. I laughed and answered, "Nothing ever changes." Feminine puzzlement appeared on her face as she quickly moved to the next display. I could tell she really didn't understand what I was getting at. To me there was very little difference between this Hawaiian idol/image and the artifacts that are sold regularly in "adult" bookstores. I'm sure some day future archaeologists will dig up the adult toys from our current society and view them as elements of our religious worship. They will be right, because that's precisely what they are and always have been. The phallus has always been the symbol of religious devotion and dedication. Professor George Elder notes,

> Phallus, like all great religious symbols, points to a
> mysterious divine reality that cannot be apprehended
> otherwise. In this case, however, the mystery seems
> to surround the symbol itself. . . . It is not as a flaccid

member that this symbol is important to religion, but as
an erect organ.[6]

The Hawaiian phallus was, of course, as described!

The first thing we learn about the phallus in the Bible is
that it is the male organ that is singled out as the unique site
for the first wound and bloodletting a man will face—circumcision (Genesis 17:10,14). Some have debated whether this first
circumcision was nothing more than a bloodletting done by
Zipporah, Moses' wife, on her own son, in order to appease
God's wrath against Moses (Exodus 4:25). Whatever the origin, the ceremony became a male marker for both the child's
dedication to God and his connection to the larger community
of faith. Circumcision throughout the Old Testament was the
sign of the Abrahamic covenant, which promised Abraham and
his descendants that they were God's people with a legitimate
claim to the real estate promised to them by God (Genesis
17:1-8). Therefore, the removing of the foreskin from the penis
was a sign of both the child's dedication to God and his being
linked to the community of Israel. It was also a symbolic recognition of God's faithfulness in the provision of male offspring
who could, in turn, produce more offspring to continue the
covenant. Circumcision, placed upon the organ of regenera-
tion, created both a symbolic and physical wound that was
a daily reminder to the boy and man of who he was. Every
Israelite, when looking at himself naked, was reminded of how
different he was from the Gentiles and for what purpose. In this
sense, his sexuality took on spiritual significance. Every time
he used his penis, he was making a spiritual statement about
who he was and who he worshiped and why. It has always
been this way, for every Jew in every culture!

In modern culture the phallus has been separated from
spiritual categories. In some of the religious circles I have traveled in, men and women view the phallus as a spiritual liability. Women sort of tolerate or joke about the phallus functions
in men, and in the church it is a rare cleric who gives any clarification to men on how the phallus should be understood and

used. The silence says as much as the overt messages. The phallus is not a spiritual subject to be discussed alongside God, the Church, and more "spiritual" doctrines.

This division of sexuality and spirituality is rather recent in the history of religious experience. In most pagan societies, sexuality was seen as an important aspect of uniting the spiritual with the physical and with the worship of gods and goddesses. In many cities, sacred prostitutes "served" at the temples in order to be the mediatrix between the gods and humans. One writer notes,

> The *hieros gamos*, the sacred prostitute was the votary chosen to embody the goddess. She was the goddess' fertile womb, her passion, and her erotic nature. In the union with the god, embodied by the reigning monarch, she assured the fertility and well-being of the land and the people. . . . She did not make love in order to obtain admiration or devotion from the man who came to her, for often she remained veiled and anonymous; her *raison d'etre* was to worship the goddess in lovemaking, thereby bringing the goddess love into the human sphere. In this union—the union of masculine and feminine, spiritual and physical—the personal was transcended and the divine entered in. As the embodiment of the goddess in the mystical union of the sacred marriage, the sacred prostitute aroused the male and was the receptacle for his passion. . . . The sacred prostitute was the holy vessel wherein chthonic and spiritual forces united.[7]

Now, certainly I am not suggesting that true sexuality and spirituality should be united in this way. After all, this was what the Apostle Paul was trying to straighten out in the Corinthian church because some of the believers were apparently still having intercourse with sacred prostitutes (1 Corinthians 6:15-20). In order to correct this perversion, he encourages the cultivation of a sexual relationship in marriage as a prevention from this abundant "sacred sex." Apparently, even the married couples had become abstinent as an over-reaction to the Corinthian extremes and had thrown the sexual relationship totally out of marriage. To this problem, Paul tells them to "stop depriving themselves," and to recultivate the sexual area of their marriage lest they be severely tempted by the culture (or Satan). In similar fashion the Church has been reacting and overreacting on the relation of sexuality to spirituality ever since.

Current Christianity cannot openly deal with or talk about the male phallus in its full sexual activity or fantasy. Much of the original manuscript for my book *Uneasy Manhood*, on the subject of men's sexuality, was edited out because it was too frank and honest, even about a Christian man's sexuality. On the other hand, modern psychology has become so sexually oriented that if a client is holding back anything of a sexual nature, he is viewed as one who has not fully disclosed, or is not being clinically honest, or must be manifesting psychological denial about his sexuality. At the same time, most secular therapists have not given much attention to the adjacent spiritual issues that surround a full understanding of the phallus. Thus, they deal with sexual addictions and dysfunctions without considering the larger and deeper connections that might relate to issues of worship, spiritual bondage, or demonic activity. Monick observes this oversight by both psychology and the Church. He writes,

> People are uneasy with the correlation of sexuality and religion. Christianity, especially has separated the two in a way that would make them appear to be irreconcilable. Psychiatry continues the disjuncture, emphasizing it with pathological labels. The church elevates religion, devaluing sexuality. Psychiatry does the opposite—elevating sexuality and devaluing religion. The union of sexuality and religion is like an electrical connection. Wrong joining leads to disaster. No joining produces no energy. Proper joining holds promise.[8]

A scriptural theology of sexuality joins them properly. I believe until the church sees men for what they are, phallic males with all their inherent spiritual tensions, it will not begin to reach men where they are living. Without proper teaching on the phallus, men will carry around in their psyches a spiritual god-hunger so mysterious and powerful that when driven underground, it will seek spiritual fulfillment only in the secrecy of motel rooms, adult videos, and in the bragging and joking about sexual exploits in athletic locker rooms. For many men in our culture, the secrecy has driven them to gay bars, topless nightclubs, and endless secret affairs. This sexual energy, which is essentially spiritual, takes place under the cover of darkness, perhaps because the Church has not shed enough light on the spiritual nature of our sexuality. Therefore, our sexual compulsions, addictions, and aberrations have become our expressions of worship—worship of a false god.

In fact one of the greatest evidences of the inherent union of sexuality with spirituality is the ritual basis for sexual addictions. One writer in particular has noted the ritualization that takes place in our sexual addictions. Carnes observes,

> For sexual addicts an addictive experience progresses through a four-step cycle which intensifies with each repetition; preoccupation, ritualization, compulsive sexual behavior and despair . . . for the addict, the sexual experience is the source of nurturing, focus of energy, and origin of excitement. It is the remedy for pain and anxiety, the reward for success, and the means for maintaining emotional balance.[9]

Whether it is the use of pornography, or the practices of peeping Toms, or the visiting of gay bars, what has emerged is that in each of these there exists a certain set ritual. One man told me his: "It always started with planning an evening away from my wife and kids. I would concoct a meeting or something and say it would probably get out late so don't wait up. I would then pick up a six-pack of beer and drink that on the way downtown. Once downtown, I would visit a hotel lounge, down a couple glasses of wine, then head directly to the gay bars. After making a contact we would go have sex wherever we could. Then I would drive home to my wife and kids. It was the same routine almost every time. It was my ritual!"

Our sexual problems only reveal how desperate we are to express, in some perverted form, the deep compulsion to worship with our phallus. We are like those Hawaiian cultic objects. We have enlarged the erect phallus and dedicated it to the gods. In time, the phallus itself becomes our god.

Many men get stuck in Phallic City, though it is a normal part of a developing manhood. It begins in adolescence and continues throughout the life span. But not always with the high level of intensity or energy experienced during the teen and early adult years. Some men, however, never quite grow up. Sam Keen observes,

> The evidence suggests that many men never graduate from the locker-room school of sexuality. . . . The frequency of date rape, the sale of girlie magazines, and the popularity of hard porn provide a fairly accurate index of how many men in their chronologically mature years are still caught in the adolescent philosophy.[10]

It becomes self-evident that unbridled sexuality becomes harmful for men as well as women. When the phallus is given over to its full-blown spiritual power without restraint, it becomes an idol. Therefore, in the sacred Scriptures God makes it very clear that the phallus, though being the symbol of God's faithfulness and provision, must be regulated, lest it become a very mysterious taskmaster.

The Phallus in Regulation

When God gave the law to His people through His spokesman Moses, His concern was not in making Israel miserable or trying to take all the fun out of their lives. Moses states God's agenda very clearly, "So the LORD commanded us to observe all these statutes, to fear the LORD our God for our *good always* and for our *survival*" (Deuteronomy 6:24, emphasis added). It was for the nation's survival as a people and for their own good that God gave the regulations and ordinances. Like any good parent, our God has His children's best interest in mind, nothing else. He wants us to not only survive as a people but also to live well.

In an AIDS-infested society this realization ought to make more sense than in the free-love and free-sex society of the prior two decades. Now even talk-show hosts, star athletes, and some in the gay community are advocating such things as abstinence, restraint, and "clean" (monogamous) sexual partners. In other words, they are trying to do exactly what our God was trying to do in the giving of the Law — regulate our sexual behavior because of the inherent potential for destruction when wrongly used. So what has God said on the subject?

The first thing noted about the phallic male in the biblical book of Leviticus is the value placed upon the emission of semen by the male. Most modern translations can't really handle what is going on in the text. The Hebrew term, usually translated "emission or discharge" by English versions, is the term *zob*. The literal meaning of *zob* is a "flow of mucous substance" (Leviticus 15:1-33).[11] It is fairly clear that what is being regulated in the text has to do with either the normal nocturnal emissions that happen to young men or to the emissions during masturbation or intercourse that fall on the bed sheets. Adding the word *seed* (*zera'*) in 15:16, as in the seed going out of a man, makes it even clearer. Without getting hung up on the details as to why certain washings or days of abstinence are required, the underlying assumption is that what happens to a man's semen is very important to God. If the circumcised penis is the sign of God's faithfulness and provision related to the Abrahamic covenant, then the regulation of what comes out of it should not be surprising. I believe this still has profound implications toward a Christian's view of sexuality. The writer of Proverbs encourages the male to seek the blessing of

God in his sexual flow (ejaculation) by rejoicing in the wife of his youth (Proverbs 5:18). The writer, it seems, is somewhat amazed that a man might think otherwise! Our sex life has great importance to the living God, even to the details of what happens to our semen.

The second most striking observation about these regulations is how God was attempting to focus on and make a very lucid statement about "sexual orientation." I use this term mainly because of the way our present culture is misusing it. Sexual orientation has become a sort of sexual smorgasbord. In the South, I used to love to go to my favorite cafeteria because they had every kind of food imaginable. It was accessible, warm, and ready to be eaten. Sexuality in our culture has become the same. Whatever you want, it's there for the taking. It's your choice. All choices are equal, one no better than another. Whether gay, bi, or straight, sexuality today has been reduced to the power of choice and however one wants to be oriented.[12]

Our God knows our hearts. He knows that without regulations we end up doing what others are doing, or just experimenting with whatever may give us momentary feelings of pleasure. All the commands, prohibitions, and exhortations in the Bible say one thing in particular—we are very prone to do a wide range of sexual things. As men, these injunctions about our sexuality seek to regulate for all times our phalli. We may think about doing many things, we may find pleasure in certain acts, but this is really beside the point. God seeks to orient our sexuality for our best interest and His glory. So what are the prohibitions?

The major prohibitions with regard to the male phallus have to do with keeping creational distinctions. The first has to do with bestiality. The biblical book of Leviticus is very clear: "You shall not have intercourse with any animal to be defiled with it, nor shall any woman stand before an animal to mate with it; it is a perversion" (18:23). Though the text does not give us a reason for this prohibition, it is a fairly consistent rationale in Leviticus that God is attempting to keep the divine creational distinctions in place without confusion. To confuse the animal-human distinction God made in creation is an abomination. Our phallus was given to us by God for the purpose of uniting with a woman, the divine gift, who was created (in one sense) to be the opening for the man's penis. For the phallus to be placed in an animal is not only a serious departure from the divine design, it can also have serious medical complications.[13]

Another prohibition found in Leviticus deals with homo-sexuality. The text says, "You shall not lie with a male as one lies with a female" (18:22; see also 20:13). Even though this is not a popular verse or subject, the current gay movement necessitates a serious but sensitive approach to the subject.

At the outset I want to say a couple of things about the gay men's movement. I have counseled gay men, I have had friends who have professed to being gay, and at almost every men's retreat or conference I speak at, I will end talking with some gay men about their unique difficulties. I am opposed to any kind of gay-bashing, and I am deeply concerned that we will be losing to AIDS a large and talented resource of human creativity, energy, and contribution that lies in our gay communities. (Heterosexuals will be lost, too.) Having said this, I must speak out of my own observation, research, counseling experience, and spiritual conviction. From this passage in Leviticus, it couldn't be clearer what God's opinion is about a man's use of his phallus. The penis has no place *in* another man. A man was not created to do with another man what he was intended to do with a woman.

Again, why does God say this? Because He obviously knew men would be put into situations where this would be a very real temptation. Whether it be men at sea for months at a time, or men in prisons, or adolescent boys playfully experimenting with each other, situations can create the temptation. The pleasure experienced in those playful moments, or the bonding that occurs through the first experience—subsequently repeated—does not change the reality of the creational order. The distinction between men and women by God's divine design must be maintained in order to have an honoring relationship with Him. The primary purpose of our sexuality is affirmed only through a relationship with the feminine counterpart in the institution of marriage.

I have often counseled gay men on my observation that even in their sexual relations with each other, they must find a substitute opening for their penis. Even though they may be thoroughly committed to the gay lifestyle, every time they engage in sex they are not only affirming their "choice" of homosexuality but also, in a more oblique way, they are affirming their creational heterosexuality in practice. For a man to have satisfactory sex he must find an opening for his penis. In rejecting the God-given opening of the woman, the homosexual merely affirms what he thinks he is denying whenever he finds an alternate opening.

But what about those men who say "God made me this way"? After one of my sessions at a men's retreat, a young man stayed long after the other men had left the room. Finally he asked if he could talk to me. We went for a long walk around the grounds of the retreat center. Where we started the walk and where we ended were two different mental places in the young man's life. When we started he said, "For years I have known that I was gay, but I have decided to be a eunuch for the Kingdom." He was basically saying, "I know I'm gay, but I want to obey God, so I won't practice my homosexuality." I asked him, "How do you know that you are gay?" He replied, "From my earliest experiences, I've been more attracted to men." His conclusion from this attraction was that God had made him that way from birth.

Most of us have heard this argument. I have looked at the evidence of hormone imbalances, and even the newer research on gay men's brains. Even though LeVay's research findings have shown that the brains of dead HIV-infected men are different (smaller) from the brains of heterosexuals, this is no proof for the theory. Even LeVay admitted his findings do not establish "cause and effect," and if they did, no one could know which is the cause and which the effect. Does the size of the brain determine homosexuality or does homosexuality determine size? No one is sure, says Joe Dallas in a critique of the born gay argument.[14] Other studies done on the general population of men have revealed that "human sexual tastes and activity are not biologically fixed, but are fluid across the life span."[15] In other words, the sexual preferences among men can change over time making the biological argument somewhat suspect.

Dr. Richard Restak, a well-respected neurologist, has shown that environment and the roles we play in it along with what we think about influence our daily hormonal levels. This in turn makes our brains different in the final (dead) analysis.[16] In my opinion, the most this "scientific" research would suggest is that certain men might have a greater predisposition toward homosexuality than other men. But predispositions are one thing, definitive sexual orientation and practice are another. I have the predisposition to be an adulterer every day! Many socializing forces interplay with whatever the biological factors are in this constellation of needs, wants, experiences, and choices.

As we continued walking I asked my new acquaintance, as I often do, to give a quick overview of his sexual history either beginning with where he is now and going back, or beginning with his first sexual experience and coming forward. He chose the latter.

For him, it was very memorable. He said, "It was when I was nine years old; I was playing with my thirteen-year-old brother, when he began playing with me down there. I felt very aroused and then he had me arouse him. I just remember how pleasurable it was. I've known I was gay ever since." I then asked him, "If something is pleasurable, does that in and of itself make it right?" As a biblically aware and committed Christian, he knew it didn't, but until we had finished our walk he hadn't taken the time to think through that first experience in light of Scripture. I asked him, "Do you think your first sexual experience was normative?" He uttered quickly, "Yes." I responded, "So you think that a man should learn about sex by having sex with his older brother?" He paused. Finally, he said, "I guess not."

Because men do not really reveal their deepest sexual experiences, fears, or frustrations, they often have no idea what is normative. We think "normative" is whatever our experience has been. One of the main characteristics of children raised in dysfunctional homes is that they have no real idea what normative behavior looks like. They may think child abuse, incest, and not talking about what Daddy does are all normative because that's all they have ever seen.

All this is to say that in counseling gay men for twenty years, I have not had one yet whom I would say had a normative childhood or normative adolescent development in the sexual arena. More often than not I have found stories of abusive, alcoholic, or absent (physically and emotionally) fathers; stories of incest or first experiences in sex forced upon them by older brothers, neighborhood men, or even friends. I sometimes find these men have had early exposure to pornography, along with devastating experiences with the opposite sex wherein they were accused of violation, or were utterly rejected or refused sexually. I agree with Leanne Payne that most of the gay issues are, in fact, major identity issues that are the result of traumatic experiences and that have created significant amounts of grief and loss in the gay's personhood. Payne writes, "There is no such thing, strictly speaking, as a lesbian or homosexual, but that he or she is simply alienated from some valid part of her/himself."[17] For men, their masculinity was stolen, so they go looking for it in other men, trying to reunite their phallus with their own lost manhood. My retreat friend who opened up his inner sexual door needs my compassion for what he lost on that innocent day with his older brother.

Another man, a successful attorney, told me how his own mother had taught him how to make love to a woman by having him make love to her. Since the day his father abandoned the family, his mother insisted he sleep with her every night. Once he began developing as a young man, his mother began to "arouse" him in the night. As a college student he turned to alcohol, and then began cruising high school activities where he could meet young teenage boys. His leverage was being old enough to buy beer. He would buy it and then try to get guys back to his room in the dorm. By the time he graduated he was thoroughly gay. His story made me weep. He was robbed of something very sacred and mysterious in that first encounter with his mother.

Another man, wrestling with sexual addiction, told me of watching his own father window-peek on his sister as she undressed at night. These were his first sexual memories as a young child. Not being able to understand why his dad was outside the window was the first pain of a robbed sexuality. In those moments, a child's sexual innocence was lost forever. The later addictions were just the perverted attempts to recover what was lost. The Bible simply calls them what they are: abominations. Our society calls them by other names: addictions, compulsions, obsessions, and disorders.

Two other areas where the creational distinctions are to be observed are incest and modesty. The biblical injunctions in Leviticus forbid sexual unions between close blood relatives and relatives by marriage (18:18, 20:11-21). Most civil laws are still based on this Judeo-Christian teaching, but since our culture has become more pagan in orientation these distinctions are no longer closely observed. The afternoon talk shows almost daily parade such relationships as "normative," or at least as one of many choices. The amount of incest taking place even in Christian homes is alarming.

The last striking observation from this ancient teaching has to do with modesty. Today the average two-hour film reveals more skin than I remember seeing throughout my entire childhood and adolescence. The cultural change during the duration of my life has been massive. I remember when just sneaking a peek at a photography magazine in the grocery store while my mother shopped was quite an emotional charge for a young boy. Today I can see more cleavage on the front page of women's magazines and billboards than I ever did as a child.

But today, even to use the word *modesty* brings forth labels in people's minds of "prudish," "hung-up," or "fundamentalist." So what was the purpose of these regulations toward modesty in the Old Testament? Not looking upon the nakedness of anyone other than one's spouse was to be enforced rigorously (Leviticus 18). One commentary on the Jewish Torah answers,

> Greek men regularly engaged in physical sports in the nude. On some special occasions young women also appeared unclothed in public. Greek sculpture idealized the nude human body. In contrast, Judaism insisted on modest attire for both sexes. This fact led to the mistaken notion that Judaism is prudish. It is in fact a question as to whether sexual interest is stimulated more by exposure or by concealment.[18]

Good question. It's easy to condemn the Arab cultures for being backward and "prudish" because of their concern to keep the flesh covered, but perhaps they place a higher value on the body than we do. They are certainly more in the spirit of what the regulations in Leviticus were trying to do than the rampant overexposure of both male and female genitalia in modern societies.

When Lieutenant Belenko flew his Russian Mig to Japan and turned it over to the American Allies, he became a prime source of insider knowledge about the Soviet Air Force. However, when I read the book *Mig Pilot*, I was more amused by his comments about American society. Having come from a country where Western films, literature, and pornography were banned, he was curious to attend an X-rated movie. With Secret Service men attached to him, one afternoon while in Washington, D.C., he visited an adult movie house. His observation was striking. He said, having heard about the rampant decadence of the West as illustrated in its obsession about sex, that he expected the movie house to be filled with both men and women. Instead, the theater was almost empty, and of the few men who were there, several were sleeping! What he says he found was not a society that was sexually obsessed but sexually bored![19] Is this what our failure to observe these basic regulations about nakedness has created? A society that is outwardly sexually compulsive but inwardly bored!

Yes, God gave us the statutes in the Old Testament to regulate the phallus and to make it very clear where our sexual focus should be. However, just as Jesus made it clear that the real locus of adultery is in the human heart (mind), so the phallus is stimulated by how the mind conceives the ultimate sexual experience.[20] The role of fantasy in the phallic man is critical to understanding his fears, frustrations, and especially his sexual compulsions.

The Phallus and Male Fantasy

Warren Farrell is a controversial writer on men's issues. But I must admit, when I first encountered his explanation of men's and women's primary fantasies, much fell into place for me. He says, "Men's primary fantasy is having access to as many beautiful women as desired without *risk or rejection*." Women's primary fantasy, contrary to much of the popular women's literature, is for that of "security and family."[21] When the most current *World Almanac* is consulted (1992), one finds that the best-selling magazine exclusively for men is *Playboy*, with a circulation of 3.4 million.[22] This small but very significant fact explains both the popularity of pornography and the addictive elements that are a part of it. Tellingly, the best-selling women's magazine is *Better Homes and Gardens*, second is *Good Housekeeping*, and third is *Family Circle*!

The real power of pornography is that it provides men with the ultimate fantasy fulfillment without the risk of emotional rejection that often accompanies relations with "real" women. In normal sexual relations, our fragile male egos are on the line, and often the slightest rejection of our advances from our wives or lovers can drive us quickly into seclusion, brooding, and hurt. Pornography solves the problem. Here there exists a seemingly unceasing supply of super-attractive, inviting women, always available, always willing; and who give the impression that each reader (viewer) is very special. *Pornographic literature plays with our minds at the deepest levels.*

This is precisely what Solomon tried to warn his own sons about in the Proverbs. This idealized woman of the night preys on the young, taking the initiative by inviting the naive to her couch, which is richly covered with colored linens and sprinkled with scented perfumes. She says, "Come, let us drink our fill of love until morning; let us delight ourselves with caresses" (Proverbs 7:18). She makes him feel special as if he is the only one in her life (7:6-23). Little does he know that she will cost him his life! So does this primary male fantasy. More will be said about this fantasy in the next chapter, but for now it must be understood that this primary fantasy is at the root of much of our phallic problems. Our phallus must be regulated according to God's Word in order to be both glorifying to Him and for us to have a satisfactory experience at this stop on the male journey. Now for a biblical portrait of a phallic man.

Samson: The Phallic Man

When I speak at men's retreats, I always throw out to the men the question "What biblical character do you see as the phallic man?" Almost without exception some biblically literate man mentions Samson. It seems fairly common knowledge among those who are honest with the text of their Bibles that Samson's fatal flaw was his phallus. He was one of the greatest judges in Israel's history and is even mentioned in the "hall of faith" passage in the New Testament (Hebrews 11:32). So the final biblical commentary on this man was favorable in spite of his glaring sexual exploits. Why? He is the example *primavera* of the phallic male who never developed beyond the sexual level of manhood.

A quick overview of Samson's life reveals a miraculous birth and sincere dedication to the Lord by his parents (Judges 13:1-5). He took a "Nazarite vow" wherein he agreed never to have his hair cut or to eat or drink any fruit of the vine, whether it be wine or stronger drink. The Bible records that he faithfully carried through on this vow his entire life. The text says that the Spirit of the Lord was upon him throughout his life (13:25; 14:6,19; 15:14). But Samson liked and fell in love with good-looking Philistine women. Apparently, Samson hated what the Philistines stood for as the enemies of Israel while at the same time being very much attracted to their women. The first time he gazed on one of the daughters of the Philistines, he wanted her simply because she looked good to him (14:3); even though God used his marriage, she became the agent for his own deception.

While covertly trying to find out the answer to Samson's riddle for the sake of her own people, his wife uses her feminine powers. She cries and says, in effect, "You hate me, and don't really love me, or you would tell me the answer to your riddle" (see 14:15-17). After seven days of this, Samson gives in and gets ripped off. This Philistine wife is then given to one of his companions. Now one would think that Samson should have learned his lesson about having his phallus determine his relations with women. Yet later he revisits his former wife and wants to have intercourse with her, but her father refuses him. Apparently knowing Samson's appetites, the father offers his younger daughter instead, saying, "She's even more beautiful" (15:1-2). In angry response, Samson destroys the Philistines, crops and goes back to his own people to recoup. After a time, he returns to Philistine territory (Gaza), sees a prostitute, and has intercourse with her. This provides another occasion for the Philistines to design an attempt to kill Samson. Twice burned, he should have learned, but he didn't.

The next event in Samson's life is his passionate affair with the Philistine Delilah. From day one he loves her, but also from day one her allegiance is obviously more toward finding out the secret of Samson's great strength than really loving him. When he won't reveal the source, she plays the same line his wife had used so successfully. Apparently these Philistine women had talked to each other! Delilah, too, uses the "if you really love me" line to get the information she needs. Samson, it seems, cannot bear being rejected by the woman he loves, and thus reveals that his uncut hair is the source of his secret strength. The rest is history. His hair is cut off during the night, his strength lost, his eyes gouged out, and he is put into a Philistine prison. When boredom gets the best of a group of partying Philistines one night, they bring Samson before them to amuse them, but Samson's hair has grown and his strength has returned. When placed between the Philistine pillars at the Gaza temple dedicated to their god Dagon, Samson pulls the entire structure upon them, avenging himself for the loss of his eyes (16:28-30).

Samson is a high testosterone, manly kind of man. He is *zakar* to the core. But apparently he never grew beyond the phallic stage. Even though the Spirit of the Lord was upon his life, when it came to controlling his phallus, he failed miserably. He was hopelessly controlled by his phallus, thus giving in to his primary fantasy — beautiful women.

As men, the phallus defines our identity. Our lives often become oriented around it. Some women, like Delilah, understand the psychology of the phallus and use it to their own advantage. The sexual power that women have over men is often underestimated, rarely analyzed or talked about among men. Yet daily, men sacrifice careers, reputations, and marriages for the phallic pleasure that women can give. The pleasure is far more than sexual. It involves the affirmation, acceptance, and praise that the phallic male so desperately needs.

Other women would like to see men become more androgynous and lose some of the phallic impulse. Some have seriously mentioned castration as a "cure" for the violent impulses in men. Verbal castration takes place daily with large doses of male-bashing heard on the afternoon talk shows. The heart of sexual violence lies with the phallus and men's perverted focus on it, so the phallus must be cut off, they say. I am equally concerned about the sexual crimes committed by men. But I don't believe that minimizing or denigrating the phallus is the answer. To be male is to be phallic. By creation we are either male *or* female. But to understand the full range of human sexuality is to understand that we are created male and female. Our phallus is made for another, and it is this sexual power that keeps the planet populated. As men we must accept our sexuality as normal, not abnormal. We must learn to worship God with our sexuality. This means learning to honor God with our phallus in the context of the restraints He has prescribed. This is for our own good. It means, whether married or single, learning to sublimate and channel our sexual passion into things constructive and generative.

Earl Wilson, a clinical psychologist, has given some excellent advice about bringing some "sexual sanity" to the phallus. He writes,

> Sanity returns when three things happen. One, we control our sexual behavior rather than being controlled by it. Two, we use sex for its intended purposes—pleasure and procreation rather than to meet other psychological needs. Three, we keep sex in its proper perspective and don't take it too seriously. . . . There is a certain type of insanity with using sex for other than its intended purposes. I strongly believe that sexual sanity comes when sex is engaged in by a man and a woman who are married and deeply committed to each other. People who engage in sex apart from these constraints run the risk of becoming enslaved to their sexuality and thus having it lose its meaning. This is a waste and approaches insanity.[23]

We never outgrow our phallus. It stays with us all our lives, even though its power may wane. The story is told of one renowned seminary professor in his seventies walking down a city street with a young student. As an attractive, perfumed, and well-groomed lady passed by the two men, the seminary student took the characteristic masculine double take. Then, realizing his esteemed professor did not even bat an eye or acknowledge she was there, the student asked, "Sir, do you finally reach a point in your Christian life where you are no longer enticed or have problems with lust?" The wise senior professor smiled and answered, "My boy, the flesh never gets better, it just gets deader!" So it is with the phallus!

CHAPTER FOUR

The Warrior—
Gibbor: The Glorious Hero

◆

*We are not interested in generals who win victories
without bloodshed . . . sooner or later
someone will come along with a sharp sword
and hack off our arms.*

CARL VON CLAUSEWITZ
On War

What is a man without his sword?

ROBERT BLY
Quoted in *To Be a Man*[1]

WHEN I WALKED into the young man's office I knew him
only as a millionaire in his late twenties. I could not miss the
obvious "motif" of his office decor, which symbolized his business and life. The walls were covered with jungle prints, and in
the middle of the wall above a large couch was a real-life photo
of a snorting, charging rhinoceros. A brass rhinoceros paper-
weight was obtrusively placed on his important correspond-
ence. On the leather couch was a rhino pillow. Noticing the
lapel on his dressed-for-success dark suit, I observed a small
14-carat gold rhino that rounded out nicely the rhino-in-the-
jungle motif of his office.

My response upon entering his office was the question
I'm sure many ask, "Why all these rhinos?" I obviously had
made his day. What I heard for the next few minutes was his
philosophy of business, the world, life, politics, recreation, and

71

even important relationships. The rhinoceros is an animal that gets raving mad, charges massively, has two-inch thick skin, and runs over anything and everything that gets in its way.[2]

After I had listened to my young friend's explanation of his rhino decor, he must have read the unimpressed look on my face. He asked, "You don't buy it?" (Everything in his life is, of course, buying or selling!) "Oh, no," I replied, "it's just that most of the men I know have had something penetrate their two-inch thick armor; and in keeping with your rhino motif, they are lying on their sides bleeding to death." Now, *he* wasn't impressed!

I begin with the rhino illustration not to condemn this young man's approach to life or business, but in fact to commend it. I see this young charger's mental posture as being right where most late twenty-something men should be. I am personally concerned today when I see young men in their twenties having already given up the rhino fight. Whether it is from dysfunctional family backgrounds, multiple job firings, or divorces, they are dead. The warrior-within has departed. To see it happening to men so young is a sad state of affairs. They have lost their sword. Robert Bly laments this absence of warriors:

> The warriors inside American men have become weak
> in recent years . . . a grown man six feet tall will allow
> another person to cross his boundaries, enter his psychic
> house, verbally abuse him, carry away his treasures and
> slam the door behind; the invaded man will stand there
> with an ingratiating, confused smile on his face.[3]

This young businessman saw himself as a warrior, hard-charging, fighting the competition, winning in the game of life, and being very proud of the victories he had won. His accomplishments in and out of the business world were symbolically displayed throughout his office in plaques, trophies, and awards. The glory of young men is their strength, whether on the football field or in the business arena.

For several years I pastored a small church on the windward side of the island of Oahu, Hawaii. Our little church was not far from Kaneohe Bay Marine Corps Air Station. Consequently, many of my parishioners were skin-headed, hard-charging Marines. During the Iran hostage crisis the base was put on alert. When this happens, a contingency of Marines are outfitted for battle and placed on the airstrip with barbed wire around them until the presidential order to go is given. During one of these occasions, a good friend of mine was put on alert for weeks, away from his family and friends, waiting for the time he would go and potentially be put in harm's way. After several weeks, the alert position was canceled. His family, friends, and church were relieved. Our prayers for the family had been answered. He was home safe again.

When I saw him I asked if he was glad to be home again. To my surprise, he wasn't; in fact, he was disappointed. He quickly educated me on the mind-set of the warrior: "A marine exists for battle—that's what we train for, that's what our lives are about, that's what the Semper Fidelis is all about." He is always ready, always faithful—to the Corps. To be faithful to the Corps meant he was ready to be first ashore and first to die! Therefore, he was disappointed. As a marine he had missed the opportunity to be what he had trained to be and to do. Any marine worth his salt would have felt the same way.

Popular Rejection of the Warrior

But this mind-set seems sick to many in our culture today. It shows to what extent our contemporary society has devalued the role of the warrior, if not the very existence of such. Battles, guns, bombs, swords, knives, blood—these are the accoutrements of the warrior, but most of these are decried as violent by women. The interesting irony is how women say they hate violence, yet love the conquering hero. If Warren Farrell is right, that the means to the male's primary fantasy (many beautiful women) is by fulfilling the primary female fantasy of having her hero or successful performer provide her home and security,[4] then the image of the warrior must not be truly condemned by women. Either women are not telling the truth, are not aware of their real feelings, or perhaps they do not want to know of the psychological violence that a man has had to do to himself and others in the process of becoming successful.

One Desert Storm wife I talked with was jubilant over her Special Forces husband's return from Iraq. However, he had the need to get some things out in the open emotionally from his time over there. She didn't want to hear it. She finally told me, "I don't care what he did over there; I don't want to know if he killed someone, or had an affair, or what. I just want our family to get back to normal." She loved the warrior but didn't want to hear of the violence the warrior had done to gain her attention and praise.

If warfare images are the toys and fascinations of men, then these are what need to be taken away from men and young boys in order to get rid of their violent natures. This is the argument often heard among women today. Even feminized men fall into the argument—if only to keep their emotional umbilical cords intact with their mothers and wives. One psychiatrist made the observation that after two full decades of anti-gun and anti-violence parenting and socialization, there is still no recognizable difference in a boy's fascination with guns and aggressive (violent) games. He writes,

> The psychology of the sixties playing on the Vietnam
> generation bred a group of parents determined both
> to minimize gender differences and to prohibit toys
> that glorified militarism. The power of androgens and
> genes confounded these optimistic parents. I have now
> observed both the "insensitivity" of pre-feminist parents
> and the "consciousness raising" of the post-feminist gen-
> eration, and can discern no significant difference between
> their male progeny, all of whom still delight in weapons.[5]

In spite of overwhelming research to the contrary, some anti-gun lobbyists, some feminists, and most of those who would totally dismantle our military under the guise of peace condemn the warrior. Warriors are labeled warmongers, baby-killers, and murderers. Operation Desert Storm perhaps has given the warrior a more positive image in the recent past, but for the most part, the warrior is not viewed positively by Western civilization. Much of what the growing men's movement in America is about is the recovery of the warrior, often to the dismay of women, especially feminists. Robert Bly, the guru of the movement, has said, "The disciplined warrior, made irrelevant by mechanized war, disdained and abandoned by the high-tech culture, is fading in American men. The fading of the warrior contributes to the collapse of civilized society. A man who cannot defend his own space cannot defend women and children."[6]

Other writers on men's issues are calling for the rediscovery of this primary image of masculinity.[7] Patrick Arnold has observed,

> The warrior is one of the most important archetypes in masculine spirituality and a central male role in virtually every society since Paleolithic times . . . yet warring is not only an occupation of great armies set off against one another across the trenches. It has become the masculine psychological paradigm for opposition to every evil: we battle disease, attack problems, combat drugs, struggle with ignorance, fight fires, and make war on poverty. Over the millennia, the Warrior has become in the collective unconscious the archetype of resistance to evil in its myriad forms; lauded by poems, songs, and stories, celebrated and sanctified by rituals, and blessed by the gods, the Warrior has come to epitomize the noblest qualities of masculinity: bravery, self-sacrifice, stamina, and heroic detachment. Today, no male archetype is under greater attack than the Warrior; in some intellectual circles the type is viewed solely as dangerous and destructive to males.[8]

Gibbor: The Hebrew Warrior

One of the most amazing things about the Bible is that it is a timeless book, unaffected by the winds of cultural change. Of the various Hebrew words associated with the concept of maleness, the word for warrior, *gibbor*, is often used and most striking. It stands unapologetically throughout the biblical text as one of the primary stages on the male journey. Men, at this stop, are warriors. Men who never discover the warrior aspect of their being are not real men. They are what Bly calls "mother-bound" boys still in need of a sword to cut their adult souls away from their mothers.[9] So what can we learn about this critical aspect of being a man?

Meaning of *Gibbor*

In Hebrew all words are built around a tri-radical base. What this means is that every word locates its semantic beginning point in three letters (consonants) that make up the main meaning. Regarding this word, the letters *g-b-r* form the meaning of all terms associated with the male warrior. It is interesting to note that in Israel today even women are designated warriors by merely adding the feminine ending to the masculine noun, making the word *gibberot*. With this in mind, the root idea present in *gibbor* is that of "power, or strength with an emphasis on excellence and superiority." The word generally has the idea of gaining the upper hand, or in another associated form, "to be prominent, important, or to have significance or be distinguished."[10]

Deborah Tannen, Georgetown University linguist, having studied the language patterns of both men and women, concluded that men and women speak and hear different languages. Her observations about how men use language confirm the warrior instinct in men, even in how we communicate. Commenting on her own marital dynamics, she writes:

> Having done the research that led to this book, I now see that my husband was simply engaging the world in a way that many men do: as an individual in a hier-

archical social order in which he was either one-up or one-down. In this world, conversations are negotiations in which people try to achieve and maintain the upper hand if they can, and protect themselves from others' attempts to put them down and push them around. Life, then, is a contest, a struggle to preserve independence and avoid failure.[11]

What this research linguist is saying about men is that they use the language of the warrior; that's how men perceive the world, engage people, and talk about any subject. And apparently it is mostly unconscious!

Gibbor is always used of grown men, never of women. In fact, to be likened to a woman is a serious putdown for a warrior (Jeremiah 30:6). Only men over thirty years old were called *gibborim* (1 Chronicles 23:3,24,27); men in their twenties did not yet qualify for the honor. The concepts of strength and the warrior are so intertwined in the biblical texts, the implication is that a warrior without strength is a contradiction in terms. The psalmist confesses, "I am reckoned among those who go down to the pit; I have become like a man [*gibbor*] without strength" (Psalm 88:4).

From this general overview, we see that the primary elements of the long-standing masculine archetypes are contained in the word *gibbor*. To be a male warrior is to be characterized by strength, competing to be superior (remember the rhino), using one's energy to be prominent, or vying to be important or to gain significance. It is almost as if the sexual energy of the phallic stage has given birth to more vocational pursuits, whereby the man wars in every area of his life. Like the successful young businessman committed to his rhino philosophy of life, men at this place on the masculine journey are very much on target. Therapist Robert Moore has observed that behind every creative artist, competent author, or successful student, there is an active warrior at work who recognizes transcendent values and relativizes temporary needs or immediate demands.[12]

It is the warrior in men that energizes them to keep going, to press toward goals, to stand their ground, to defend their personal and corporate values, even to the point of risking self. As men we war in business, in sports, in marriages, in our conversations, and with our political agendas. Ministers I have known, including this one, have waged war for the correct construction and articulation of truth and a "proper" understanding of the gospel. Graduate students compete for stipends, scholarships, honors, and straight A's. Gay men war for what they consider to be their civil rights and "war" to gain acceptance in the military.

Is the warrior instinct inherent in the nature of men dead? No! Even though contrary socialization has tried for several decades to obliterate the warrior. Again, look at the best-selling men's magazines. If men's natures are illustrated by the magazines they buy, one can see that the warrior aspect is not dead. It was noted earlier that *Playboy* is the best-selling men's magazine in the U.S. What was not noted at that time was that numbers two, three, four, and five all depict some aspect of the warrior. As listed in the 1992 *World Almanac, Sports Illustrated* is second, *American Legion* third, *Field and Stream* fourth, with *VFW* coming in fifth. All of these have circulations of over two million. Even the other men's magazines that make the top one hundred best sellers have common warrior themes. *Money, Outdoor Life, American Hunter, American Rifleman,* and *Golf Digest* all have the images of survival, hunting, challenge, power, competition, and winning.[13]

The male warrior instinct is not dead because it is intrinsic, woven into the fabric of our being as men. I contend this is a normal and natural stop on the male journey and not one to be despised or devalued by either men or women. It is a vital aspect of being male and without it we are not the males we ought to be. I thank God I had a dad who taught me how to fire a gun, to not be afraid in the woods, to respect life but to be willing to shed either animal or human blood for my own survival or for the protection of my family. Many men today are so abused and defeated by life that I am afraid they don't have enough of the warrior left in them to defend themselves, their families, or their societies. For them, the place to begin is to see that our God is very much a warrior.

God as Warrior

I remember well the antiwar rallies of the 1960s. Thousands of college students were in the streets yelling slogans like "Hell, no, we won't go" and marching with raised placards. One particular placard was present at most of the rallies. It picked up the biblical command "Thou shall not kill." Even as a nonChristian I was biblically aware enough to know that somehow God Himself had sanctioned His people to take human life both in war and via capital punishment. Therefore, the biblical command in the antiwar context never really struck me as legitimate. When we take the time to look at the term *gibbor*, we find that God Himself is a warrior. He is characterized by His warrior strength in the words of the prophet Jeremiah, "There is none like Thee, O LORD; Thou art great, and great is Thy name in might [*gibbor*]" (Jeremiah 10:6). God as a *gibbor* is seen in the psalms as one standing and fighting for righteousness, justice, lovingkindness, and truth. The psalmist says of Him,

> Your arm is endued with power;
>> your hand is strong, your right hand exalted.
> Righteousness and justice are the foundation of your
>> throne;
>> love and faithfulness go before you.
>> (Psalm 89:13-14, NIV)

It is by God's warrior strength that He saves and vindicates humankind (Psalm 54:1-4, 20:6). So united is the relationship between God's warrior strength and His very character that God's name Yahweh becomes identified with *gibbor*:

> Therefore behold, I am going to make them know —
> This time I will make them know
> My power and My might;

> And they shall know that My name is the LORD [Yahweh].
> (Jeremiah 16:21)

The Jewish Passover memorializes what God did in the land of Egypt in order to get His people, Israel, out of bondage and into the Promised Land. In the Passover we celebrate God as warrior. It was God who fought for His people, bringing the plagues on the Egyptians, parting the Red Sea, and miraculously defeating the armies who came up against the infant nation. One commentator observed, "One thing the Exodus does not require is any military violence on the part of the Hebrews . . . Moses' 'arsenal' does not include a single bona fide 'weapon'—no swords, spears, bows, or knives, much less chariots and horsemen. It is Yahweh who fights!"[14]

The point of this is very straightforward. God is not a passive, immobile, unconcerned God who would never lift His holy finger in violence. He is a God who fights for His people to liberate them, save them, protect and sustain them. All the attributes of the warrior are His. The Scriptures present God as strong, powerful, and willing to use His power to achieve His righteous purposes in the world. Often, from our modern perspective, God does things that seem unjust, even violent, but that is what the life of the warrior is all about, even for God. So also for the One who comes in His name. Personally, I am very thankful that God both has fought for my salvation in the past by offering up His own Son and will fight again to right all the wrongs committed from the beginning of the human race. I'm glad that my Savior, Jesus Christ, is also a warrior.

The Messianic Warrior

I am skeptical of anyone today who tries to argue the case for a holy war. I am a military chaplain serving in the Air Force reserve in the Air National Guard. As a chaplain I serve as a noncombatant. Even though the noncombatant status doesn't guarantee immunity from war zones or getting killed, it does mean that it is not my job to take human life. Yet, I do believe that God has given the power of the sword to established governments. This divine authorization gives the power to governments to take life whether in war or by capital punishment (Romans 13:1-4). Good government seeks to use the sword in ways that are ethical and moral. Honorable presidents will convey a sense of justice (just war) in their use of power. But I do not believe that just war equals in fact a holy war.

A holy war is when God tells us to fight in His name. The Scriptures, I believe, record only two holy wars: the conquest of Canaan under the command of Joshua, and the final war of the world, where Christ Himself will wage war against all the armies of the earth (Revelation 19:11-19). All others I would have difficulty calling holy. War is anything but holy. To call it holy in this modern nuclear age is to border on blasphemy—maintaining that something is clearly of God when it is not. This, of course, is the Muslim view of holy war, or *jihad*. The only wars that are truly holy are where God Himself has made the determination, and I do not believe we can know that in this present age. Therefore, the only true warrior for God is the One who sits at His right hand and knows perfectly His Father's will.

We see in the promises concerning the future Messiah that one designation to be placed upon Him will be *El Gibbor*, or the mighty-warrior God. In the often-quoted Isaiah passage (9:6), one of the several names for the predicted Messiah is warrior, *gibbor*. What is interesting in this passage is that this name is listed alongside eternal Father and Prince of peace. In other words, being God is not inconsistent with being a warrior, and being a warrior is not inconsistent with being the Prince of peace. Warfare is not in opposition to peace! What has been the Air Force's motto for years is equally true of the Messiah: "Peace through strength." God's ultimate representative, His own Son, the Messiah, is a warrior fighting for the truth, laying down His own life for His Father's cause. One day He will mount His white horse and slay the armies of the world and establish a perfect, lasting peace (Revelation 19:11-21). This is as much a part of Christ's redemptive work as His dying on the cross. The warrior must be willing to put his life on the line, in order to accomplish anything worthy of redemption. This willingness to risk one's life characterizes those national warriors and heroes who protect their societies.

Gibbor as National Warrior and Hero

Throughout the Old Testament, the most common usage of the term *gibbor* refers to the experienced veteran of combat or the hero status achieved from accomplishing spectacular feats of bravery and making a name for oneself. *Gibbor*-strength is needed to win a race (Psalm 19:5) or a war (Isaiah 36:5); the term is also used of the human/angelic offspring who were mighty men of old and made a name for themselves (Genesis 6:4). Nimrod was known as a mighty hunter and warrior before the Lord (Genesis 10:9). One can be known as a *gibbor* merely by achieving status for one's ability at drinking wine and strong drink (Isaiah 5:22). This particular passage by no means places a benediction on the drunken warrior, but merely reinforces the necessary element of "greatness at something" that characterizes the warrior.

The *gibbor* can also be a man of standing as obtained through his material wealth. King Menahem of Israel extracted money from his people for the Assyrian king by taking it from all the *gibbors* of wealth (2 Kings 15:20). Boaz was such a man, a *gibbor* of great wealth (Ruth 2:1). When the Philistines were giving King Saul a real headache, he went on an active recruiting campaign whereby any *gibbor* he saw was immediately enlisted into his service (1 Samuel 14:52). When Joshua made preparations for going into the land of Canaan, he instructed all the wives and children to remain on the Moab side of the Jordan, but it was the valiant *gibbors* who would cross the river to do battle (Joshua 1:14). In fact, all of Joshua's army who were fully armed for warfare were called by the plural, *gibborim* (Joshua 8:3).

Two of Israel's judges are called *gibbors*: Gideon and Jephthah (Judges 6:12, 11:1). We know Gideon made quite a name for himself in destroying the pagan altars and fighting the Midianites with an elite corps of three hundred *gibbors* (Judges 7).

However, it took the reign of David to advance the concept of the *gibbor* to that of a standing militia and a handpicked, elite corps of warriors to protect the royal court. David organized a special cohort, much like America's modern Marine Corps embassy guards, as his finest thirty. They were handpicked by David's commander of the army, Joab (2 Samuel 10:9), quartered in the special "House of the Heroes" (Nehemiah 3:16, NIV), and given special honor on the basis of their military achievements. (See the list of heroes in 2 Samuel 23:8-23, called mighty men, or *gibborim*.) In modern terms, these were the most experienced, combat-ready, and well-decorated special forces of their day. When the throne passed to David's son Solomon, they pledged their unwavering support to the new king (1 Chronicles 29:24). They were truly the "semper fi" marines of their day, pledging their support to their commander-in-chief no matter who it might be.

Solomon apparently continued the practice of having the royal elite guard. The number of his *gibborim* grew to sixty. In the love sonnet attributed to him, he comments on their "parade dress" appearance:

> Look! It is Solomon's carriage,
>   escorted by sixty warriors [*gibborim*],
>   the noblest of Israel,
> all of them wearing the sword,
>   all experienced in battle,
> each with his sword at his side,
>   prepared for the terrors of the night.
>   (Song of Songs 3:7-8, NIV)

They were his elite guard leading the way on his wedding day, guarding from any possible terrors during the night. Their armor was polished, their swords sharp, and their march smart.

Such is the pride of the few, the brave, the elite. The pride of the warrior is hard to explain, but it is the same pride seen in athletes as they cross the finish line, score a touchdown, or slam a victory dunk. We see the same pride in a businessman who closes a deal or in a man who finally kisses the girl of his dreams. It is all there, the honor, the tribute, the significance, the pride of winning, of just being a part of an elite group.

What is confusing to those who have never really experienced the combat of business, athletics, or warfare is how glorious the conflict is. In my book *Failure to Scream*, I noted how there exists an addiction to action because of the adrenaline rush that takes place when one's life is on the line. The "high" of killing is one of the least understood and most ignored phenomena in many circles because of its radical implications for human nature. On a broader scale there are other attractions to conflict. A philosophy professor reflected upon his World War II experience and concluded:

> What are the secret attractions of war, the ones that have
> persisted in the West despite revolutionary changes
> in the methods of warfare? I believe that they are, the
> delight in seeing war as spectacle (being where the
> action is), the delight in destruction and the delight in
> comradeship. . . . It is no wonder that General Robert E.
> Lee once remarked to his staff, "It is well that war is so
> terrible—we would grow too fond of it."[15]

Anyone who has been in the fray knows that therein lies an unexplainable feeling of being most alive, most needed, and part of something very important. When shared with comrades in arms, the bonding is powerful and virtually impossible to replicate in peacetime.

This camaraderie of brothers is severely missing today. I have known many former military personnel who, as committed Christians, still yearn for the *esprit de corps* they experienced in secular military settings. Somehow the church has not been able to create a Gideon's Three Hundred, or a David's

Thirty, or the Twelve of Jesus Christ. Perhaps we don't really believe we are at war or that our brothers in the faith are dying. Without this honorable group spirit, and the sharing of pain with other *gibborim*, the rewards of the warrior are pale. In fact, as we found in Vietnam particularly, the bravery documented had very little to do with "serving one's country" or following orders; the extreme acts of bravery were done in the interest of the corps. As one commander put it, "Our men were not willing to die for their country, but they were willing to die for their buddies, and did!"

The Bible does not condemn the warrior, but merely assumes the warrior is a part of the routine expression of manliness. God the Father and Christ are examples of what it is to be a warrior. As men it is vitally important for us to embrace the latent or rejected warrior within ourselves, not only for our own development, but also for the sake of our society and the Church. The warrior never serves himself. He is a servant of the king and his commander. Likewise, we must know what and who it is we serve. To be seen as a virtue, the physical power of the warrior must be in the service of a larger view of masculinity.

To be the warrior is not the goal of manhood. It is only a necessary stop on the male map on the way to full maleness. Some in the past have equated the warrior with the fullness of masculinity, but this is not true. It is an important part of our manhood, but it is not the whole. A view of masculinity that is nothing more than unrestrained power is no masculinity at all. Power must always serve the higher values of the King. Scriptural insight would suggest the true aspect of the warrior that should be developed is the spiritual warrior, and this involves far more than just being tough, strong, or having to win.

Gibbor as Spiritual Warrior

If King Solomon is identified as the Koheleth (preacher or collector) in the book of Ecclesiastes, then he offers a very wise perspective concerning the warrior. In spite of the fact that he personally placed so much trust in his own military might, Solomon says, "*Wisdom* is better than [warrior] strength" (Ecclesiastes 9:16, emphasis added). The psalmist goes even further, saying,

> He does not delight in the strength [*gibbor*] of the horse;
> He does not take pleasure in the legs of a man.
> The LORD favors those who fear Him,
> Those who wait for His lovingkindness.
> (Psalm 147:10-11)

Isaiah declares that a man's real warrior strength lies in such things as repentance, resting in one's salvation, and in the quiet trust of God (Isaiah 30:15). God Himself reaffirms this idea through the prophet Jeremiah: "Let not a wise man boast of his wisdom, and let not the mighty man [*gibbor*] boast of his might, let not a rich man boast of his riches; but let him who boasts boast of this, that he understands and knows Me" (Jeremiah 9:23-24).

These passages clarify the nature of the true warrior. He is not the warmonger or baby-killer that the Vietnam-era radicals made the warrior out to be. As one actively serving in the National Guard, I greatly value the image of our national hero—the "logo" of the guard is the Minuteman, with one hand on his plow and the other on his rifle. To me this is the true warrior, especially in light of the source from which the historical symbol was derived. These warriors were not professional soldiers as were King George's elite corps. These were farmers who united to build and defend a fledgling republic born out of their faith in God and their quest for religious and political freedom. These warriors were husbands, fathers, brothers, and sons. They all had their property and values on the line. They bore arms to defend what they believed in, and when the conflict was over they went home to built communities, schools, and families. They weren't much of an army by European standards, but they won. I contend they won not because they were such good military warriors, but because they knew their own limitations and placed their faith in God.

I don't live far from Valley Forge, where General Washington almost lost his ragtag army to the cold Pennsylvania winter. About five miles from the park stands Valley Forge Military Academy. In the front of the chapel is a stained-glass image of Washington praying in the snow. Farther north and east is Washington Crossing, the place where the general, in the dead of winter on Christmas Day, crossed the Delaware and surprised the sleeping, hung over British troops at Trenton. Every time I stand there and look at the size of the Delaware River, I am amazed at the chutzpah of Washington. How could he have moved his army across this very wide river, without freezing or starving to death, and without detection? To me it is both a miracle and a tribute to the real nature of the warrior, one who trusts in God!

The warrior does not trust in his own abilities, although he does maintain a healthy perspective on them. His genuine commitment, allegiance, and trust is in God. This is good news to the man who has not had a significant male role model in his life. Our fatherless generation can learn much about being a man by studying God's Word and seeing God as the virile Warrior, and in so doing place its trust in God. The true warrior does not trust in his own strength but in the strength of the Lord. This is the true manliness inherent in the spiritual warrior.

The psalmist is also a realist and admits the *gibbor* can use his power for malevolent causes and become a violent man, full of evil. Though these attributes are not the ideal for the true warrior (Psalm 52), they do raise the very real possibilities inherent in the warrior psyche.

Basically, the spiritual warrior is the warrior who trusts and finds his refuge in God rather than in his own strength or material possessions. The psalmist again says, "Blessed is the [*gibbor*] who has made the LORD his trust" (Psalm 40:4). In contrast, Jeremiah observes, "Cursed is the [*gibbor*] who trusts in ['*adam*, mankind or the creational-fallen man]" (Jeremiah

17:5). Even though the warrior may be strong physically in his own might or achievements, the mental configuration he must have to be a spiritual warrior is one of not trusting his own abilities. The wealthy *gibbor* who trusts in the abundance of his riches is not only foolish but evil (Psalm 52:7). What is good is for the warrior is to take refuge in the Lord (34:8). The ultimate spiritual reward for the *gibbor* is not in the honors, decorations, or medals he may obtain, but in the children God gives to him (127:4). This gives a profound twist to the concept that the warrior is set in opposition to the family. In fact, throughout history it has been the warrior who has always gone to battle to defend his family from threat. This passage underscores the divine value that is placed upon the family, and upon the value of bearing children. Children are the *gibbor*'s real strength, they are his arrows!

In one very interesting passage, the defeated, suffering Job is told by God "to gird up his loins as a warrior would do preparing himself for battle" (Job 38:1-3). This was not to do battle with God, for that is precisely what Job had been doing throughout the book. In wrestling with the questions of God's goodness and eternal purposes, Job had asked on numerous occasions to have God speak directly to him. But when God finally spoke, He asked Job to gird up his loins (literally what is between the loins!) as a warrior would, in order to receive the words that God had for him. This is powerful stuff.

The implication as I see it is that I need to respond to God as a warrior when He has a harsh word for me. For three chapters God lays it on the line concerning Job's pushing the divine envelope (boundaries). In short, God puts Job in his place by reminding him of who he is, but He also asks him to receive the admonition as a warrior would. The warrior, as any good marine will tell you, responds, "Yes sir," salutes smartly, does an about-face, and marches out briskly to carry out the orders of his commander. No debate, clarification, or response, just "Yes, sir." That's what a spiritual warrior does with God. The divine/human line is never crossed or debated. The warrior lets God be God, and knowing his own position before the

Lord, salutes smartly and goes on to carry out God's task in the world.

In this regard, King David is the supreme example of the spiritual warrior and the *gibbor*. No matter how his victories were won, he credited his military accomplishments to God and sang praises to Him (1 Chronicles 29:11-14).

David: The Premier Warrior

So much has been written about David, the greatest of Israel's kings, I feel humbled trying to give a quick summary of his life. But the profile I hope to provide is one gained by looking at David's life through the lens of the warrior. The story of David actually begins with the slaying of the Philistine *gibbor*, Goliath (1 Samuel 17:4). We all know this story well. David is ashamed that there are no true warriors courageous enough to go up against this uncircumcised Philistine. Whether in jest or out of desperation, King Saul places his own armor on David, and out goes the young boy. But David uses the weapons of his own trade, those of a shepherd. With the accuracy of his sling, this young boy brings down the giant *gibbor* with one shot and returns to camp as the man, the *gibbor*, the warrior. His victory is celebrated throughout Israel (1 Samuel 18:6), and as a reward, King Saul gives David command of one thousand men (18:13). Now David is a military commander, a *gibbor* in charge of other *gibborim*.

After the death of Saul, David becomes king, and his first act is to throw down a warrior-like challenge. The first in his command who will kill a Jebusite shall be the new commander. Joab jumps at the chance, kills a Jebusite, and obtains the command (1 Chronicles 11:6). During the reign of David, he builds Israel's ragtag militia into a large standing army, very similar to what George Washington did. David equips them for war, and then wages constant battles with the surrounding nations in order to gain strategic and territorial advantages (1 Chronicles 12:22-40, 18:1-3).

Some of these warriors' actions went far beyond merely killing the enemy. We find David decapitating Goliath and cutting off body parts with a saw after one of his later victories (1 Samuel 17:51, 1 Chronicles 20:3). The violent-bloody realism of battle is found in the life of this *gibbor*, who also loved God, wrote poetry, played stringed instruments, and danced. Is this surprising for the image of a warrior?

It seems even Barbara Walters was a little surprised by the "humanness" of the warrior when she interviewed "Stormin'" Norman Schwarzkopf. As the commander of Allied Forces in the Persian Gulf War he was viewed as a gruff, strong, matter-of-fact kind of guy—the premier Four Star General caricature. However, to Barbara's amazement, she saw a man who wept when asked about being away from his family, who admitted he was scared before every battle and that it took no courage to order men to battle. The real heroes are the foot soldiers who face off with the enemy. By all counts, however, Schwarzkopf is a true warrior who combines love of opera and family with the required blood and fierceness of combat.[16]

David is called *gibbor* by King Saul's royal court, and puts the warrior label on himself in his own poetry: "To the faithful warrior [*gibbor*] You [God] show yourself faithful" (2 Samuel 22:26). The heading introducing David's last words also reveals this warrior self-image: "The oracle of David son of Jesse, the oracle of the man [*gibbor*] exalted by the Most High" (2 Samuel 23:1, NIV).

When I teach on the life of David I like to ask my audience what in their opinion was David's greatest sin. Since David is called "a man after God's own heart," this becomes a fascinating question because David was anything but perfect morally. Usually, the answers I get very quickly are his adultery with Bathsheba; having Uriah (Bathsheba's husband) killed in battle; or the deceit he illustrated through both of the above. But rarely does anyone mention the one sin that David confesses himself that almost caused the entire nation of Israel to be killed by God (2 Samuel 24:15). The sin was in David's idea to muster all his warriors throughout Israel and have them counted (24:2). Even Joab, Israel's faithful commander, thought it was wrong, but King David prevailed.

Consequently, God sent a plague upon Israel that began taking an extreme toll on the populace—seventy thousand dead! Finally, David admits he has sinned in this act and God calls off the plague. Now we know from the parallel passage in Chronicles that Satan was behind the idea in David's mind (1 Chronicles 21:1), but the question remains as to why God thought this act of numbering was so evil. To us it seems so trivial.

The answer may lie in Joab's final calculation as given to David. We are told, "Joab gave the number of the registration of the people to the king; and there were in Israel eight hundred thousand [*gibbors*] who drew the sword, and the men of Judah were five hundred thousand" (2 Samuel 24:9). Wow, 1.3 million warriors in David's army! Upon hearing the news, the text says, "David's heart troubled him." That's a polite way of saying, "He was smote in his heart by the numbers." Apparently, he had no idea up to this point how large an army he could wield on the battlefield. As a military officer myself, I know how important it is for every commander and commander-in-chief to know exactly how many troops or aircraft are mission-capable on any given day. The numbers of mission-capable aircraft in the Air Force is a carefully guarded, very classified, statistic. Numbers are power. Numbers are the power of self-reliance and capability.

Once David realized the size of his army, he knew he was no longer in the same position to trust God. Now there would be the lurking evil tendency to trust in his own military strength rather than in the Lord. For David, it was his gravest sin, while at the same time showing us what kind of man he really was. Few men today would call recognizing one's own strength and abilities an evil, but apparently David did. He was the true spiritual warrior. He warred not in his own strength but in the strength of the Lord. In his single-handed charge against Goliath he declared, "The battle is the LORD's" (1 Samuel 17:47).

As illustrated by David we see a downside to the life of the warrior. To be a successful warrior, blood must be shed. The blood of enemies is always mixed with one's own blood. The life of the warrior, necessary as it is for developing manliness, has its liabilities.

We see the liability in David's life at the point of his greatest desire. More than any pursuit in his life he desired to honor God by building a permanent structure for the Ark of the Covenant. He appropriated all the natural resources, employed the skilled craftsmen, and personally financed the project with his own money. God had personally given him the plan from which to build it. But when it came down to the actual construction of the Temple, in which the Ark would be housed, God told David the bad news. He was a man of war, and a man who had shed much blood (1 Chronicles 22:8, 28:3). Therefore, David would not have the privilege of seeing the dream of his life fulfilled. Solomon, his son, would build the Temple. Apparently, houses dedicated to the service of God were not to be built by men of war. Warriors have their place, but not in certain kinds of spiritual service. The very blood that David shed in conquering Israel's enemies became for him the stumbling block preventing him from building God's house.

There exists a certain irony here in the life of the warrior. The warrior is a much-needed stop on the male journey. It is the place where young men grow up considerably. I've seen it happen almost overnight in military boot camps, in graduate education, in young men standing up to their parents for the first time, or in standing up to a boss on the basis of principle. It is when the urge to fight or flee presents itself, and deep within the male personality the voice that normally said "flee" grows strong and surprisingly says, "fight." The fight matures, the conflict ages, and the drawing of psychic blood develops the young phallic male into a *gibbor*, a warrior.

Men must win some battles to prove to themselves that they are men. In past cultures this was ritualized but, unfortunately, today men must fend for themselves and almost declare themselves men. But it still involves blood, risk, and sacrifice. Just as in times past, whether through circumcision or other cutting of the body, the passages to manhood involve the shedding of some blood. For city boys, there are no more rituals, no more calling out the boys from the villages of women, no more going out into the woods to kill one's first lion or bear. Even most Jewish men I know have told me that, although they found the bar mitzvah meaningful, it did not bring the recognition of manhood—or the treatment as a man—they had hoped. They still felt they had to prove something long after the ceremony. So we must find our warrior courage in other ways to consider ourselves men. Today, that may happen the first time we stand up to our fathers, or ask our mothers to stop criticizing, or stop allowing our family members to manipulate us. It will probably vary with each man.

I remember two substitute puberty rites with my own father. One was when I was twelve years old. Being general manager of Beech Aircraft Corporation, my dad had a single-engine, V-tailed Beech Bonanza for his use. We spent many hours in this plane together. I can still vividly remember the day we taxied the plane to the runway, and then after revving the engine and doing all the pre-fight, he pulled a pin out of the "stick" and swung it over to my side of the airplane. His only words were, "I think you're big enough to take this off." I was twelve years old, but that day my dad saw me as a man. Even though I was scared to death, the belief that my dad trusted me with not only this airplane but also his life gave me a surge of warrior courage. I reasoned: "If my dad thinks I am old enough, then I must be." I pulled back on the throttle, raced the plane down the runway, and pulled back on the stick. When we were airborne I felt like I had had my bar mitzvah. That's the day my dad looked upon me as man.

But there is another marker on my own male journey, this one years later. I was married with two children at the time. My parents were getting on in years, my dad retired, and I suggested that we all go out to dinner. Knowing my dad and his "manly" devotion never to let his kids pay for anything, I made arrangements with a restaurant to have everything billed to my credit card before we arrived. After a delightful meal my father began looking around for our waitress. When my dad finally caught her eye, she came over. He asked her for the bill, but she replied it had already been taken care of. With surprise he asked, "By whom?" She pointed at me and said, "Him!" I had outfoxed him. He politely looked at me and announced, "I guess you're old enough to buy your mom and dad dinner."

That's the night I *felt* like a man in my dad's eyes. That's the night I killed the bear and passed the test. Even though to you, my readers, this may sound strange, it took all the warrior courage I could muster to pull this off with my father. Wherever the bears are in our lives, we must call forth the warrior within us to kill them. We must trust God with the outcomes and risk psychological or even physical injury to self or others — all in order to become men. *What is a man without his sword?*

Bly again notes what happens when men as fathers lose the warrior instinct. He observes,

> As fathers lose touch with the warrior, fewer fathers give any modeling beyond the copper bridge (being conductors of others' feelings) when faced with female anger. "My father never stood up to my mother, and I'm still angry about that." Hundreds of men have spoken that sentence at gatherings. Sometimes all that would have been necessary would have been for the father to stand up for his boundaries, or for the limits of verbal abuse, and simply say firmly, "enough." If the father cannot set limits to the mother's raging . . . or loss of temper, the children turn into copper wires.[17]

One of the most encouraging things about all men's groups I have experienced is how they rally around another man to help him pick up the sword, whether in his work, his marriage, or dealing with his own demons from the past.

But here is the irony. The warrior does not necessarily fit the gray-headed man. Remember our original proverb: "The glory of young men is their strength, and the honor of old men is their gray hair." To see men fighting battles they no longer need to fight is not only inappropriate for the season but sad.

One man I worked with in the ministry was like that. He was much older than me, his silver-gray hair was already present, but he was still a warrior. Every conversation, every issue in the church became a call to arms and an opportunity for warfare. Immediately, he became the warrior, dividing the positions into two camps, going on the offensive to show the opposition where they were wrong. As a young man, I liked his warrior approach. It was strong and virile. I thought it was the right way. I admired his convictions, his drawing lines in the sand, his courage to take on deacons or elders and refuse to compromise. I thought it was the right way. I thought it was the only way. Now I'm not as convinced. As I have watched men war in business, the military, the ministry, and graduate school, I wonder what all the fighting is about.

The challenge of being a warrior is twofold: knowing what to fight for, and knowing when to quit. Neither is easy to learn. We certainly need warriors for the truth, to fight for the spiritual values in our society before they become extinct. But we also see many who war needlessly, or war for causes that are far removed from the category of "worth dying for." Usually it will take a very tragic loss or wounding experience in the life of a man to move him out of the warrior perspective on the male journey.

The warrior never fully leaves us, but given enough time, the warrior fights enough battles to become severely wounded. The slings of arrows of outrageous fortune finally find their target in us. The wounding experience plunges men into radically new and uncharted territory. The journey is dark, scary, and uncomfortable. For most of the men I have worked with and confessed my own journey to, we agree on one profound point. This next stage on the male journey is one we would like to have omitted or detoured around. When we are thoroughly stuck in Woundedville, we are convinced we are lost and will never find our way back to the main road. If you have some of the warrior courage left in you—read on!

The Wounded Male —
Enosh:
The Painful Incongruency

◆

To be a man is to bear wounds and wear scars.
PATRICK ARNOLD
Wildmen, Warriors, and Kings

I'm wounded but am not slain,
I will lay me down for to bleed a while.
JOHN DRYDEN
"Johnnie Armstrong's Last Goodnight"

I MUST HAVE been all of five years old, but I still remember the experience. Driving with my grandfather to his favorite fishing hole is one of those childhood memories that I retain to this day. I remember his huge, late-forties car, with the cane poles sticking out my passenger-side window. I remember the way the river looked and smelled, and how the birds were chirping. I remember his tackle box with all the fishing paraphernalia in it, and the little .22-caliber gun, just in case he had to shoot a snake or something.

This was a big day for me. Granddad Riley (my mother's dad) taught me to bait a hook that day. Or I should say, I watched *him* bait my hook and then his and throw them both in the river. After a while, I pulled in my line and found my worm was nibbled away, so I put the hook in front of him. "Nope," he said, "it's time you learn to bait your own hook." Bravely but nervously I tried meticulously to place the worm on the hook. Granddad did it with such ease, but it's more difficult when the slimy worm is in your own hand. With one final desperate stab I speared the worm completely—completely through its wiggling body and into my finger. There was no blood as I remember, but panic filled my little mind as I realized what I had done to myself. There the hook was, barb and all, deeply planted in my finger with the worm still moving trying to gain his freedom.

The panic I felt in my mind finally reached my mouth and I cried, "Granddad!" Tears streamed down my cheeks, as I started to cry. In one swift action, Granddad said, "Be quiet, men don't cry," and unemotionally reached into his tackle box and pulled out some pliers. While I clenched my teeth, he pushed the barbed part of the hook further into my finger and out the other side and then broke the hook off. The remaining part of the hook came out the original wound. Then the blood flowed. He took out his handkerchief (real men always carried them back then) and wrapped it around my finger. "This happens when men go fishing," he explained.

It was my first wound. It was also one of my first experiences as a boy with another man on the subject of wounding. It was all there. Wounding is a part of a man's life, but when wounded we don't cry. We clench our teeth, wipe our tears quickly, and cover the wound as tightly as possible. The message from my first male mentor was clear from the top down: Real men don't cry. Women suffer wounds the same as men, but they can cry, scream, and yell, and it's all considered normal. We men have to watch the painful barbs move through our lives without flinching. After all, the warrior is tough. But sooner or later, given enough wars, even the best of warriors end up being wounded.

While researching my book *Returning Home*, on the Persian Gulf War, I was told by one army airborne trooper, "The day I killed my first Iraqi something died in me." A fairly successful executive revealed, "If I had known life was going to be so tough, I don't know if I would have signed up for it." Another explained, "I think I'm finally realizing what the lack of a father has really done to me." It's no surprise that the founder and guru of the emerging men's movement, Robert Bly, is an adult child of an alcoholic father. Whether in his seminars or books, he roots the men's movement in the repressed pain in men's lives, the pain they feel as the result of being wounded by life. In order for men to discover what manhood is all about (finding the "wild man" in Bly's frame of reference), they must descend into the deep places of their own souls and find their accumulated grief.[1]

Men act out some of the unconscious pain they have accumulated with violence. In fact, Sam Keen suggests that the unhealed wounds of men are more devastating upon other men than upon women in our society. He writes,

> Men are violent because of the systematic violence done to their bodies and spirits. Being hurt they become hunters. In the overall picture male violence toward women is far less than male violence against other males. For instance, the F.B.I. reports that of the estimated 21,500 murders in the United States in 1989, two-thirds of the victims were males.[2]

So much literature has emerged on the wounded male recently that it seems to represent a new awareness for men. However, the men's movement writers have gone back to ancient literature in an attempt to find metaphors in which to frame our understanding of the masculine experience of woundedness. It is as if for several generations men have not had fathers and mentors in their lives to teach them how to handle woundedness, and counselors and writers have had to go elsewhere to find suitable stories or models that include the concept. What drives much of this current literature are the very ancient stories of the male experience. Robert Johnson bases his understanding of the masculine experience on the legend of Parsifal and his search for the Holy Grail. Johnson believes the Grail myth speaks of masculine psychology. In it, the Fisher King, who is the king of the castle, has been wounded. His wounds are so severe that he cannot live, yet he is incapable of dying. He groans, cries out, and suffers all the time. Johnson builds the theory that for boys to become men they must—like the Fisher King—become aware of the deep wounding within. He writes,

> It is painful to watch a young boy become aware that the world is not just joy and happiness, to watch the disintegration of his childlike beauty, faith and optimism. This is regrettable but necessary. If we are not cast out of the Garden of Eden, there can be no heavenly Jerusalem.[3]

The wound is a wound to his maleness, a fatal mortal wounding that seems incurable. Being a warrior makes us as men have kingly views of ourselves. The Fisher King can't accept his wounding, just as we have trouble accepting our wounds. Like the Fisher King, we moan and groan about those wounds until we find a way to work through them. In the meantime, those around us suffer and ask, "When are you going to get over this?"

For Carl Jung, this wounding is critical to the development of a deeper masculinity. He sees the worst of it coming from what a boy or man does to himself. It is only through wounding that a man becomes aware of many of the unconscious elements in his being. Jung states,

> The torment which afflicts mankind does not come from outside, but that man is his own huntsman, his own sacrifice, his own sacrificial knife. . . . The deadly arrows do not strike the hero from without; it is himself who hunts, fights, and tortures himself. In him, instinct wars with instinct; therefore the poet says, "Thyself pierced through," which means that he is wounded by his own arrow.[4]

Jung uses the metaphor of the male species wounding himself through various forms of self-destructive behaviors.

For Jung, this is the only way that men come to grips with the reality that they are no longer the heroes they imagined in their youth. They must grow up as men by becoming "painfully aware" of their deep-seated wound.

In a very imaginative approach to men's issues, Robert Fisher writes a somewhat humorous but convicting satire of a knight in rusty armor. A desperate knight, in search of his true self and in order to find such, must rid himself of the rusty armor in which he is encased. The armor that had served well the purposes of the warrior has become a prison in normal "peacetime" relationships. In order to begin the process of ridding himself of his heavy armor, the knight must encounter his own pain. Of the knight, Fisher says,

> The knight had lived in his armor for so long he had forgotten how everything felt without it. It took a tremendous blow on his helmeted head by the smith with an ax, or by Juliet with the nearest vase, before he noticed even a twinge of his own pain. And since he had difficulty feeling his own pain, the pain of others went unnoticed as well.[5]

I like this story. Many men, myself included, have had to have the proverbial blow to our heads to jar us sufficiently and bring us to our senses about ourselves. Through this wounding we encounter our constructed defenses that have kept us protected but isolated from the rest of the world. Sam Keen states more bluntly: "From the beginnings of recorded human history to the present day the most important tacit instruction boys receive about manhood is: Masculinity requires a wounding of the body, a sacrifice of the natural endowment of sensuality and sexuality."[6]

What Keen is alluding to is the almost universal history of primitive societies whereby the males went through a formal puberty rite that required the experience of pain and wounding of the body. Circumcision is a permanent wounding of the body that reminds the Jewish (and now

Gentile) male that he is what he is—male. Other societies have their tatoos or cutting of the body. American Indians bond through blood. Young boys even today emulate the old rite of cutting the fingers and mingling the blood to become "blood brothers."

When I was initiated into a fraternity in college we had our own somewhat frightening and painful initiation ceremony into the brotherhood. The military has boot camp whereby, to be included in the community of soldiers, one must endure the painful discipline of physical training, the verbal abuse of drill instructors, and the losing of all privileges that were associated with the "younger civilian life."

From our first hours of maleness until we become adult, pain seems to be the doorway to manhood. Thus, the wounded male experience is common among most civilizations, but contemporary Western men have either denied or forgotten it. Consequently, when pain arrives we Westerners struggle against it. The emerging men's movement may be, at its roots, the attempt to reframe the wounding experience for men and give it a new and more honorable meaning.

Some would say this new awareness about men's wound-edness has created an openness for men to *talk* about their pain without the stigma that was attached to men's pain in the past. Most of us have been like my grandfather: "Men don't talk about their pain, lest we appear sissies or feminine." But from the viewpoint of biblical literature, the experience of the wounded male is not uncommon. Carl Jung did not dis-cover men's woundedness. Neither did Sam Keen or Robert Bly. Woundedness has been one of the profound experiences found in all the ancient literature. The Holy Scriptures are no exception. The Bible honors it as a normal stop on the male journey, an experience common to many biblical characters. *In fact, in the biblical motif, when a man encounters his wound he encounters and wrestles with God.* As such, the wounding experience for men in the Bible gives us a very helpful portrait of the male experience, and one from which men can emerge with newfound insights about life, God, and ourselves.

Enosh: The Wounded Male

After Israel's King David selfishly and sexually used Bath-sheba, who was the wife of one of his most faithful soldiers, the child they conceived fell sick and eventually died. The Hebrew word used to describe the sickness suffered by the male baby is the word *enosh*. The child's sickness and weakness reveals the meaning of *enosh*. In its etymological development, the word conveys the idea of "being weak, feeble and sometimes incurably weak or sick."[7] This Hebrew expression for the word *man* describes his mortality, calamity, frailty, and fears (Isaiah 17:11, Jeremiah 17:16).[8] It is most often used in the book of Job, which records the extreme violence and emotional wounding that the loss of life, property, health, and wealth did to one undeserving of such. Job illustrates wounding in its most severe form, and the resultant struggle a man encounters in trying to understand how God, his faith, and his relationships can continue to have meaning in light of such intense pain.

Job's struggle to make sense of his woundedness offers a rich commentary about the *enosh* experience. He says, "Is not [*enosh*] forced to labor on earth, and are not his days like the days of a hired man? . . . So I am allotted months of vanity" (7:1). He says to God, "So Thou dost destroy [*enosh*'s] hope" (14:19). Job's experience is that of the wounded male, the man who has been wounded by life's misfortune but, being a man of faith, knows that God somehow is behind the misfortune. In this sense, a relationship with God only complicates the problem. The man without faith merely deals with the calamity, but the man of faith must wrestle with God over it. Philip Yancey has explained, "The alternative to disappointment with God seems to be disappointed without God."[9] Either way, one is disappointed. But disappointment with God is sometimes more difficult to accept than dealing with suffering without God. Factoring God into the equation only heightens the struggle.

Job cannot accept the fact that he has personally done anything in his life to deserve such extreme malevolence. Why would God either directly or indirectly through natural calamities (it doesn't really matter which way to the one who has lost everything) allow Job to lose all his children, property, wealth, and finally his health? In the process of trying to understand his losses, even Job's own wife and friends turn out to be poor comforters. They suggest that Job should curse God and die (2:9) or confess the secret sins of his life that are the apparent just cause of such extreme tragedy (11:13-19). The reality is that Job never knew why he suffered, therefore the meaning of his wounding has been lost in the contradictory feelings of wanting to believe in a benevolent God and hating God for allowing such injustice to befall him. Job's struggle with woundedness is his struggle against God in an attempt to prove his innocence.

The psalmists also speak much of this *enosh* kind of man. King David writes, "As for [*enosh*], his days are like grass" (Psalm 103:15). "What is [*enosh*], that Thou dost take thought of him?" (8:4). Moses prays, "Thou [God] dost turn [*enosh*] back into dust" (90:3). In these poetic sections, the psalmists view the male experience as one of experiential mortality, frailty, and limitedness. Sometimes this *enosh* experience manifests itself in violence and hostility toward mankind. When King David was seized by the Philistines at Gath, he prayed, "Be gracious, O God, for [*enosh*] has trampled upon me; fighting all day long he oppresses me" (56:1). Even in receiving God's good gifts of food and drink, there is a subtle reminder that we as men are limited beings: "Wine . . . makes [*enosh's*] heart glad . . . and food . . . sustains [*enosh's*] heart" (104:15).

These passages suggest that the *enosh* experience indeed includes awareness of one's mortality, frailty, and weakness. In this regard, the experience is not a negative one but rather normative for a biblical view of manhood and maleness. Given enough time, the journey of the masculine experience will lead us to some kind of wounding that confronts us with our most basic condition. It is in the wounding experience that I learn that I am not God, nor a little god, nor even a little bit like God. It is more the experience of wondering how or why God might have anything to do with me at all.

Now, my women readers may ask at this point, Isn't this true of women as well? Of course, women experience wounding in just as many ways as men do. But the main thrust of this chapter deals with why this normative experience is so difficult for men to accept, talk about, and heal themselves from. On this point, both the biblical material and the contemporary literature are amazingly close. From my study of the word *enosh* and my reading about men's issues, along with my counseling of men, I can draw four conclusions about male woundedness. Male woundedness means we as men experience a very strange, often unexplainably deep, mortal wound. It also means we begin to encounter in ourselves deep loss reactions. Wounded men also experience a profound alienation from God, often mixed with a certain incongruency of the soul. For many men there are additional experiences of hostility and violence. But the wounding experience begins within the deep recesses of the masculine soul.

Woundedness: The Deep Mortal Wound
It's one thing to observe that something is wrong, but trying to figure out what the "thing" is, is more difficult. Many have observed that all is not well with men today. But what is at the core of the sickness? One astute clergyman observed:

> There is a "tear" in the masculine soul—a gaping hole or wound that leads to a profound insecurity. The German psychologist Alexander Mitscherlich, has written that society has torn the soul of the male, and into this tear demons have fled—demons of insecurity, selfishness, and despair. Consequently, men do not know who they are as men. Rather, they define themselves by what they do, who they know, and what they own.[10]

What is it that has torn the masculine soul? It would certainly be easy to blame society, or the women's movement, or even the failures of our own fathers. But I believe placing blame on these players is a superficial way of looking at the problem. Each of the above may have had their distinctive contributions to the tear. But fundamentally, the wound is mortal—meaning a death experience. The wound is therefore profoundly spiritual and theological.

As I have analyzed this fledgling men's movement, I have found a movement in search of a spirituality. As such, the issues men are addressing are perhaps more theological in nature than those of the women's movement of the sixties.

From the understanding of *'adam* presented in chapter 2, we observed that men, though created in the image of God, are primarily fallen creatures. We are fallen in the sense that we are no longer what we were created to be. Created to be immortal, we no longer enjoy life on this planet apart from the experience of death. Once upon a time our first parents tried to expand upon their God-given creational limitations, and wound up tasting evil in its most deceptive form. Thus the experience of mortality entered their being and the rest of human history. But mortality apparently is an afterthought, an intrusion, an interference, a foreign and alien addition to our souls. It's not *supposed* to be there and somehow we know this within ourselves at very deep levels.

As a pastor, it has always amazed me how little my parishioners thought about, or wanted to think about, death. Mortality sermons are not very popular in a youth-oriented society. Even the most biblical of Christians still seem to live more for the American Dream than seriously preparing for their own death. I'm not sure I'm any different! Even those confined to serious illness struggle to accept the final implication of their illness—death. Elisabeth Kübler-Ross was the first to market the reality of what her research revealed about the death and dying process, namely, that psychological denial is the first of several normal grief reactions. Why is the denial of our own death experience the most fundamental, and first, reaction to terminal illness? Death is the most basic thing about human existence. If so, why do we fight it and believe it will never really take its toll on us?

Sitting on that riverbank with my granddad, I had my first

encounter with death — my own. I may have seen others bleed or cut themselves, but this was *my* finger. It was my finger with the hook in it, my finger that was bleeding, my blood, my wound. It was the first of many. Fortunately, my wounds have not been as severe as those of other men I've known. But every physical and psychic wound is one more small foretaste of death, one more taste of our own mortality. The more and greater the wounding, the more the death experience. Every time we feel pain, something has died within us.

Daniel Levinson has written extensively about the midlife experience for men. He sees this period in the life cycle as a growing realization of one's own mortality and death:

> Every man in the Mid-life Transition starts to see that the hero of the fairy tale does not enter a life of eternal, simple happiness. He sees, indeed, that the hero is a youth who must die or be transformed as early adulthood comes to an end. A man must begin to grieve and accept the symbolic death of the youthful hero within himself, and how he might be a hero of a different kind in the context of middle adulthood. Humanity has as yet little wisdom for constructing the "portrait of the hero as a middle-aged man." That archetype is still poorly evolved. For many reasons, then, at 40 a man knows more deeply than ever before that he is going to die. He feels it in his bones, in his dreams, in the marrow of his being . . . more years now lie behind than ahead.[11]

The male midlife "crisis" has certainly been well documented. I believe I've been in it for over ten years now, maybe more. Perhaps the main aspect of this crisis that has been largely ignored is what normal aging does in terms of wounding the male. According to recent studies, men probably experience life with their bodies more than women, who experience life more emotionally and communicationally.[12] Hence, the deterioration of the physical abilities and attractiveness may indeed be the continuing experience of the mortal wound that we know deep down will eventually kill us.

The experience of midlife wounds many men. For many it may be the loss of jobs or loss of marriages. For others it might be the giving up of dreams and ambitions. For some, it is the frightening realities created by the diminishing hopes of rehabilitation. Either a Vietnam vet learning to cope with life as an amputee or a recovering alcoholic who sees life as stale and lifeless without alcohol would suffer such hopelessness.

The growing reality of woundedness in younger men is very sad to see. Warrior strength, once valued among women, is being put down and condemned as violent by some mothers and teachers. Alcoholic fathers, dysfunctional families, divorce after one or two years of marriage, and multiple job firings are all wounding men at earlier ages. At men's conferences and retreats, more and more young men are coming up after my sessions and telling me their stories of abuse, aloneness, chemical dependencies, and inadequate relationships with women. Some take desperate leaps for young men and reveal their guilt and anxiety about being gay or about being straight and addicted to sex or pornography. Many of these are in the church but feel no one there would understand or be supportive. Therefore, they bury their wounds and bandage their bruises with phony smiles but wrestle with gaping holes in their souls.

My reply to them is, "Your wound is honorable; your wound is a normal part of male development. Life is not over. This wound may be the entry point for new wisdom and power; it may be the voice of God. Now we need to figure out what it means and how to move toward healing in order to keep you on the masculine journey. We need to help you find a way out of your inappropriate response to some abnormal event or circumstance in your past." It's but a momentary stop on the map of manhood.

Sam Keen believes all men are in some sense war-wounded. As such we have developed well-honed psychological armor that allows us to keep on functioning while not really healing. He writes,

So men, the designated warriors, gradually form "character armor," a pattern of muscular tension and rigidity that freezes them into the posture that is appropriate only for fighting—shoulders back, chest out, stomach pulled in, anal sphincter tight, testicles drawn up into the body as far as possible, eyes narrowed, breathing foreshortened and anxious, heart rate accelerated, testosterone in full flow. The warrior's body is perpetually uptight and ready to fight.[13]

The wounded warrior needs to begin to own the feelings he experiences, just like the American soldier in Iraq who very quickly identified what he was feeling about his own sense of loss in killing another human being. But then, we as men have difficulty recognizing these deep loss reactions in ourselves. Gordon Dalbey says, "We are lost males, all of us; cast adrift from the community of men, cut off from our masculine heritage—abandoned to machines, organizations, fantasies, drugs."[14] I'm not so sure that all men are lost in the male experience, but I do know that many men are for the first time becoming more aware of the woundedness they have experienced in jobs, failed marriages, addictions, and their own families of origin. They are beginning to grieve over what was lost when they were wounded. They are beginning to experience the appropriate deep loss reactions.

Woundedness: Deep Loss Reactions
If men find significant male meaning in being the warrior and being phallic, then anything that defeats us in these two areas brings about a profound sense of loss. We reason in our minds: "If my reason for being is to be the warrior, and warriors are no longer in vogue or the warrior in me has become wounded, then I no longer quite know who I am."

Several years ago I represented the United States Air Force at the International Conference on Wartime Stress held in Tel Aviv, Israel. At the conference, the Israeli mental health corps presented papers on what they had learned in their many wars. In opposition to the way we had treated our wounded in Vietnam, the Israelis had developed a different approach. In Vietnam, we evacuated our wounded out of the war zones as quickly as possible. It sounded like a good, sensible, medically efficient thing to do. Not so, said the Israelis. Their first goal is to keep the wounded with their combat units and buddies for as long as possible and do everything they can medically for the wounded at the front. In Vietnam, once the soldier was airlifted to a medical hospital, he was immediately stripped of his uniform and placed in the required hospital gown. Not so in Israel. They leave the uniform on, so when the wounded wake up, they still wear the uniform of the soldier. The results shared by the Israelis at the conference put our Vietnam experience to shame. *They valued the warrior even when wounded.* They wanted the wounded warrior to still think of himself as a warrior, even when limbs were amputated and there was significant loss of human functioning.

Think of how many vets there are in the U.S. sitting in VFW and American Legion posts sharing their war stories about when they really were alive. The very way they talk about the past reveals their remorse in the present. They haven't moved on in their masculine journey. Their last stop on the male map was with wounding. Will their journeys end there? They are still wounded, still experiencing some very deep-seated loss reactions. To not experience grief reactions when wounded is what psychologists would consider sick. But for men to confess what they feel and embrace their grief is not easy. Warriors don't show pain.

Job, in the Bible, had been a warrior. He had it all: wealth, a large family, a supportive wife, a large estate, friends, and good health. Then one day a cruel fate hit Job. The same way one cruel bullet, car accident, job phase-out, or spouse walking out may hit us in one swift emotional disaster. In only a day, it seems, a life can be ruined. The normal response to such is an overwhelming sense of loss. Why? Because much *has* been lost. Saying to oneself, "It was just a job" or "I'm better off without her" or "At least I'm still alive," doesn't make the pain and sense of loss go away. These reactions are just trite little﹒ phrases invented by someone who obviously hasn't entered into the tragedy of human realities. When we are wounded by life, we feel remorse for what has been lost, and we begin to live in a romantic past when things were better. The response is normal. This is exactly what Job did. Notice his remorse over what he once had:

> Oh that I were as in months gone by,
> As in the days when God watched over me; . . .
> As I was in the prime of my days,
> When the friendship of God was over my tent;
> When the Almighty was yet with me,
> And my children were around me;
> When my steps were bathed in butter,
> And the rock poured out for me streams of oil! . . .
> When I took my seat in the square;
> The young men saw me and hid themselves,
> And the old men arose and stood.
> The princes stopped talking,
> And put their hands on their mouths; . . .
> For when the ear heard, it called me blessed. . . .
> My glory is ever new with me,
> And my bow renewed in my hand. . . .
> And dwelt as a king among the troops,
> As one who comforted the mourners. . . .
> But now those younger than I mock me, . . .
> And now I have become their taunt, . . .
> And now my soul is poured out within me;
> Days of affliction have seized me. . . .
> I cry out to Thee for help,
> but Thou dost not answer me; . . .
> Thou hast become cruel to me.
> (Job 29:2,4-9,11,20,25; 30:1,9,16,20-21)

Being at the place of woundedness, Job romanticized about when he had it all—back when he was in the prime of life, when he had respect of men and the favor of God. But with the wounding of his body came the wounding of his spirit. Even God was remote. With this normal grief response we are taken to the next characteristic of the wounded male experience: the experience of creaturely alienation and incongruency.

Woundedness: Alienation and Incongruency
Cesar Vallejo, the Peruvian poet, records, "On the day I was born, God was sick."[15] This gripping, blunt phrase reflects the sense of alienation even from God that Vallejo feels. The alienation is experienced as an incongruency. I love this word. I first learned it in geometry class. There are congruent triangles and noncongruent triangles. Congruent triangles are triangles whose angles match each other. In other words, they fit; there exists a balance or harmony in the angles of the triangle. When a man is wounded by the blows of life, the wounding throws his sense of balance off. The angles are now out of whack. Most distressing of the human angles that no longer fit is the one with God. Man and his God, once intimate friends, no longer seem to agree. For the Christian, the agreement established between God and man through Jesus Christ no longer seems experientially valid. The experience of the wounded believer with God is that of distance, alienation, and of a God who seems no longer present or active in one's life.

Philip Yancey recounts a conversation with a friend with whom he had shared much about relationship with God. Yet, through woundedness they had come to different conclusions about God:

> When I had first met Richard, he was like an estranged lover in the early stages of separation and divorce—from God. Anger smoldered in his eyes. But when I saw him five years later, it was clear that the passage of time had mellowed him. His passion would still break out as we talked, but mingled with wistfulness, or nostalgia. He could not put God completely out of mind, and God's absence made itself felt, hauntingly, like pain from a

phantom limb. Even if I didn't bring up matters of faith, Richard, still hurt, betrayed, would circle back to them.

Once he turned to me with a puzzled look. "I don't get it, Philip," he said. "We read many of the same books, and share many of the same values. You seem to understand my doubt and disappointment. And yet somehow you find it possible to believe, but I don't. What's the difference? Where did you get your faith?" My mind sped through possible answers. I could have suggested all the evidences for God: design in creation, the story of Jesus, proofs of the Resurrection, examples of Christian saints. But Richard knew those answers as well as I, and still did not believe. . . .

It was during this conversation that I realized there are actually two cosmic wagers transpiring. I have focused on The Wager from God's point of view, The Wager as pictured in the Book of Job, in which God "risks" the future of the human experiment on a person's response. I doubt anyone fully understands that wager, but Jesus taught that the end of human history will boil down to the one issue: "when the Son of Man comes will he find faith on earth?" The second wager, reflecting the human viewpoint, is the one that Job himself engaged in: should he choose for God or against him? Job weighed the evidence, most of which did not suggest a trustworthy God. But he decided, kicking and screaming all the way, to place his faith in God.[16]

The experience of alienation is a normal part of the grief process. Such extreme incongruency with God during this time can lead to new understanding of the mystery of God, and a new respect for His mysterious ways.

Woundedness also accounts for much interpersonal grief. This grief is experienced in the alienation we feel toward other people, even the ones trying to help us. Asaph was one of these. Asaph was David's and Solomon's choir director. He had the job of putting David's meditations to music. Can you imagine that?

I call the psalms of David the musings of a manic-depressive! David's psalms are either all praise or all depression. He is either singing joy to God or calling upon God to judge the wicked who oppress him! Asaph got to put David's mood swings to music. I'm sure when he saw David walking into his office in the royal court he didn't know if it was to be a praise hymn or a dirge. At any rate, Asaph had seen it all, and done it all. Yet apparently, the prosperity of the wicked at one point in his life had become a wounding experience for Asaph. He was ready to throw in the towel of his faith (Psalm 73:1-2); he seriously questioned the value of continuing his practice of ritual purity because it seemed to be valueless in terms of material prosperity (73:13). The alienation he experienced from God and others, he finally admits, was derived from feeling like a wounded animal (73:22).

Anyone who has ever seen a dog struck by a car can easily see the imagery here. I have often stopped to see if I could do anything for an injured dog. About the time I get near the animal, it snarls at me, or worse, snaps at me in an attempt to bite me. This is the way Asaph says he was before God and others. He was senseless, embittered, and pierced with an uncontrollable hurt. The result is that he snapped at anyone who tried to help him.

Animals do have a certain amount of sense in their woundedness. When hurt, they try to remove themselves from the scene and isolate themselves in the woods where they can privately lick their wounds and buy themselves some time to heal. It's instinctive for animals. Perhaps we share some of this primal instinct. We men tend to isolate, buy time to nurse our woundedness, and don't want anyone to come near us, even spouses, counselors, ministers, or other loved ones who deeply care for us. This reaction is often viewed as not wanting help or rejecting the help of others, but I would say the reaction is distinctively characteristic of the wounded male. It is a grief reaction. It is a man's way of dealing with the profound sense of loss he feels no matter what caused it. Until the experience can be incorporated into a larger sense of meaning, the man can very easily remain "stuck" in his woundedness, only to lick his wounds the rest of his life. But the reaction itself is normal, perhaps a God-given grace to buy the time he needs to find perspective and meaning.

Just as the wounded animal can begin to strike out at those who come near to give aid, so men can externalize their pain and manifest hostility, even violence, toward others.

Woundedness: Hostility and Violence
When I was first writing this chapter, the Los Angeles riots had erupted in response to the Rodney King beating verdict. The city was aflame and talk show after talk show paraded expert opinions before the American public. I particularly appreciated one very educated, scholarly opinion, which best summarized the violence. This guy took a completely different tack than the other panel hosts. I don't remember his name but this is the essence of what he said: "The issue of the L.A. riots is not white power versus black power, but the complete powerlessness of inner-city problems, both black and white." Women researchers have concluded that the problem of rape is not a problem reflecting men's power over women, but men's sense of powerlessness. The only alternative left for them to gain a sense of power is by abusing and using women. To talk of men's power is to miss the point. Men feel powerless and end up acting out this feeling in a violent way. But the lack of power men feel appears to be a power issue to women. They think men need to have power over women. The reality is, they have been so reduced to subhuman categories that the only power they have left is the power of abuse and violence. This is what I believe we saw on our TV screens in L.A.

In a very controversial book, George Gilder writes,

> If young men are estranged from the leadership of society, any society faces a threat from its young men. Today in America the best example is the ghetto, where youths readily express far more respect for the Mafia than for any American public institution and where the

women and elderly all too often cower in their apartments for fear of the hoodlums who rule the streets. But throughout history, alliances between military officers and male groups of mesomorphic thugs have always emerged when the established leadership lost its hold on the public.[17]

Gilder roots this thug response in the male sense of powerlessness and his gravitating to the lowest level of masculinity, that of violence, not only toward women but also toward other men and ultimately against himself. He notes, "A man who cannot attain his manhood through an affirmative role resorts to the lowest terms of masculinity. What can he do that is exclusively male? He consults his body. He has a [penis]. But he is a failure and no woman wants it. He has greater physical strength and aggressiveness. He uses it."[18]

Wounded by society or circumstances, by parent or spouse, the hostile male feels powerless and so strikes out. The hostile spirit is rooted in woundedness. Even Job turns his woundedness outward. He screams,

I will speak in the anguish of my spirit,
I will complain in the bitterness of my soul. (Job 7:11)

He [God] has stripped my honor from me,
And removed the crown from my head.
He breaks me down on every side, and I am gone;
And He has uprooted my hope like a tree.
(Job 19:9-10)

I am convinced many men in our society today are lashing out at women, at society, at bosses, even at God—all because they do not understand the wounding experience. They cannot find it on the superficial cultural map of masculinity. Woundedness is not a valid experience for these men; it is not in their categories of acceptable maleness. It feels foreign and must be fought against or denied. As long as this myth about woundedness persists, men will not continue to develop along the male journey. They must begin to see that out of woundedness comes significant healing, meaning, and growth. In fact, a very mystical, spiritual power is born in male weakness. One study of an ancient dysfunctional family may illustrate the point.

Jacob: The Wounded Male

If all the ideas associated with the word *enosh* could be illustrated, they might best be found in the life of the biblical patriarch Jacob (Genesis 25:19–33:20). The story of Jacob reads like a modern case study of a dysfunctional family. In this sense, Jacob illustrates a young man having been severely wounded by a dysfunctional family system.

Even in the womb, there was sibling rivalry and brotherly struggle as to who would be born first and thereby receive the providential patriarchal priority of firstborn (25:22). Esau, a real man's man, covered with hair, emerged first, but his brother Jacob was hanging on to his foot, trying even from birth to dislodge the family blessing. Esau, the hairy one, was his father's pride and joy, loved to hunt, and enjoyed wild game (25:27). Jacob, on the other hand, was a momma's boy who would rather be in the kitchen trying out some new recipe with Mom (25:29). Consequently, from the earliest days, we see classic parental favoritism developing. Isaac loved Esau, while Rebekah loved Jacob (25:28).

Favoritism eventually turns to outright protectionism and deception. Rebekah figures out a way for her favorite to steal the legal birthright from Esau (27:5-13). Having pulled off the scam with Mom's help, Jacob then has to live with a guilty conscience for years. The remainder of his recorded experiences are filled with fear and the extreme necessity of having to affirm to himself that he is legitimately blessed before men and God. The long-term effects of his woundedness come to a head when he hears that his long-distance brother is coming to see him accompanied by four hundred men (32:6). Jacob is afraid to meet Esau and develops a strategic plan to appease Esau's perceived wrath.

Having sent all his family, servants, and livestock across the river, he is finally alone with his pain and ready to meet God. Tradition holds that the one he encounters is an angel of God. Now I am convinced that only a warrior who has been wounded by a dysfunctional family would think that he could wrestle with an angel of God and win! But Jacob thinks he can win and almost does. In fact the text says, "When [the angel] saw that he had not prevailed against him, he touched [dislocated] the socket of [Jacob's] thigh" (32:25). We are never told what motivated Jacob to wrestle this stranger. But his experience is the experience of many men. Many of us wrestle with strangers in the night as we try to find the blessing we never had.

This elusive blessing becomes an important metaphor on the male journey. Jacob is so insecure in his standing with God and his brother that he must prove he can gain the upper hand with whomever comes across his path. Because his only blessing is the one he stole through deception and parental favoritism, he wrestles with God in the night to gain a more secure blessing. Only a naive young man would think he could wrestle with angels and win without suffering some sort of additional wounding. Sometime during the night, the angel finally blesses him, but only after his whole hip has been dislocated. When the sun rises, Jacob is left limping on his thigh (32:31).

The wound suffered from wrestling with the angel provides the key to the needed reconciliation with his brother. The next day, as his brother Esau approaches, Jacob is no longer in the prime of youthful strength. He is limping. He meets his brother not in accordance with his strength, but out of his weakness. Later, the Apostle Paul reveals that this weakness is the key not only to a developmental view of manhood but also for the entire Christian life, for "power is perfected in weakness" (2 Corinthians 12:9). The metaphor of Jacob reveals that the wounding experience need not be negative, but can be a time of meeting and wrestling with God. From the experience of wrestling we are in a better position to see what life is all about and what is important. Though we may limp the rest of our lives because of the wounding, at least it has new significance, a significance that places a frame of positive meaning around the experience.

Purple Hearts for Broken Spirits

The warrior has been glorified in both ancient and modern societies. Honoring wounded warriors has been more difficult in our enlightened American culture. We have devalued both the role of the warrior and his wounds. When I meet military personnel in their forties or beyond, I first notice their rank and then take a quick look at the ribbons on their chest, which detail an individual's career distinctions. I always look for the green and white Vietnam campaign ribbon. Then I look for the purple and white ribbon representing the purple heart awarded to those wounded in action. At least the military has learned something that civilians may still have trouble accepting. Being wounded needs to be recognized, praised, and awarded.

I realize purple hearts do not in any way make up for the pain and loss suffered by many American vets, but at least the award symbolizes merit and value. It is the recognition that the country not only values the warriors who do its dirty work, but also those who end up wounded in the process. In the absence of cultural markers from fathers, wives, or institutions, we as men need to affirm and value the wounds ourselves. Perhaps only in the circle of the fellow wounded can purple hearts for broken spirits be awarded. In reality, only one who has been wounded can honor the wound in others. The celebration does not have to be with trumpets and salutes. Sometimes it is only the quiet, even nonverbal, recognition that another man understands. Women, it seems, want to talk it all out, complete with all the details. But with men, the wound is almost honored more by not saying much about it. For those who have shared similar pain, just being there is enough, often acknowledged with just a nod or quiet facial expression.

Pulitzer prize winner Lewis Puller, a double amputee from Vietnam combat injuries, recounts his road to recovery.

In talking about his first Marine Corps reunion held after the dedication of the Vietnam memorial, he writes:

> For the next two hours we sat and received the attention and love of men who, though strangers, shared a kinship with me that surpassed time and place. Forged as it was in the bloody crucible of Vietnam, it was unnecessary for me to give my name or to offer justification for my physical condition. (In a wheelchair with no legs.) This blessed band of brothers and I had shared the worst and the best that life had to offer, and in our reaffirming our connectedness, words were, for the moment, super-fluous. . . . "Welcome home, brother" were repeated as Toddy (his wife) and I made our way to a sitting area near the bar; no response seemed required of me. I was at last back among the men who had fought with me and pro-tected me in the now-distant rice paddies and jungles of Vietnam, and I felt safe and at ease in their company.[19]

For men to survive their wounding, I believe they need to feel safety among men who have also suffered pain. The pains we experience as men are our bar mitzvahs, our tribal bondings, our marks of manhood. They need to be honored and valued by both men and women. Perhaps the only true wisdom is the wisdom that is born in pain. For us as men, *Enosh* City may become a stifling dead end on the male map, or it can be just a detour on the masculine journey. My hope is that with the help of some honest brothers who acknowledge our pain, we can move on and obtain an even greater perspec-tive on life. We can begin to move toward wholeness with a greater sense of direction and purpose in life.

From our time of wounding we can emerge as rulers of our own souls again, not so willing to sell out our precious lives for such small price tags. We now know who we are and are ready for the next destination on the masculine journey.

CHAPTER SIX

The Mature Man—
Ish: The Reborn Ruler

◆

No one gets to adulthood without a wound.
ROBERT BLY
Iron John

I never thought I'd lose,
I only thought I'd win.
ELTON JOHN
"The Last Song"

What are you doing here, Elijah?
THE LORD, SPEAKING IN A STILL VOICE
1 Kings 19:13

AT THE TIME of this writing, trying to meet my publisher's deadline, I have isolated myself in the mountains of North Carolina. In an A-frame overlooking the community of Blowing Rock, I experience the Christmas holiday under a blanket of snow and ice. I have been listening to the travel advisories all day. They forecast freezing rain and sleet all day long and urge anyone not having to be on the road not to venture out. However, a call from my literary agent changes my perspective. He wants to meet me at Woodlands Bar-B-Q, a local hangout known for good food and "down-home" country pickin'. I say, "Great, a chance to get out." I jump into my car and try to conquer the incline of the driveway. I start sliding. In typical male fashion I will not be denied this challenge. I back up, rev up the engine, downshift to second gear, and hit the gas. I'm almost all the way up the driveway when the front-wheel drive hits the icy blacktop. My front wheels spin out of control and the front of the car veers to the right, ending up parallel with the driveway. The car is now precariously perched over the incline's dropoff. Putting the car into "park," I go back into the house and call my friend to admit my "incompetence" and failure to beat the storm. *Now what do I do?* I think. *I could call AAA for a tow job or I could just leave the car and wait for a thaw.* I decide on the latter.

As I sat there that night by the fireplace thinking about the day, it came to me that my trying-to-get-out-of-the-driveway experience was why men end up dealing so poorly with the wounding experience. We are not really prepared to be defeated by life. We expect to win, whether it be in football, our marriages, our businesses, or getting out of an icy driveway. You are not considered a real man if you expect to lose. It's not American and certainly not masculine.

The second insight that came to me while warming myself by the fire was that we as men don't always listen very well. I had listened to the travel advisories all day. When I walked to my car, I almost slipped twice because the ice was so bad. But somehow this data got blocked out by my desire to eat barbecue and master the challenge of the icy driveway. It was almost as if the warnings and travel advisories were for someone else. They obviously didn't apply to me, because I am Bob Hicks, a real man who won't be stopped by a little ice or inconvenience! As Elton John so passionately proclaims in his song dedicated to men dying of AIDS: "I never thought I would lose, I only thought I would win." As men, we have a certain conditioned or innate sense of invulnerability that says we will never be harmed, never be fired, never go through a divorce, never get cancer, and never come to the point where we view life as total disaster. Therefore, when we find ourselves dying of AIDS, or without a job, or facing a bland marriage, or just being demoralized by our fractured families, we cave in and feel very out of control. We so pride ourselves in the mastery of life. And when it is gone it seems we become slaves to our wounds. Our response to such experiences catches us off guard. After all, we didn't have fathers who modeled how to go through the wounding experience. Most men don't even want to talk about it, much less help some other man through it. But this is the good news: The spirit can be reborn; the pains experienced in woundedness can be birth pangs anticipating the next destination on the male journey.

Maturity springs only from adversity. We know this from the brother of Jesus, who says it clearly: "Blessed is the man who perseveres under trial, because when he has stood the test, he will receive the crown of life that God has promised to those who love him" (James 1:12, NIV).

I don't know how many times as a child or adolescent I heard, "Grow up, Bob!" I find myself now saying this to my teenage son—"Grow up, Graham!" It is like someone somewhere has clearly set forth what "grownupness" looks like. In telling a man to grow up, what are we saying? What model of manhood or maleness do we have in our minds that suggests some image of maturity upon which we can measure adult male behavior? I don't suggest I have the answer, but I do believe that whatever maturity is, it is developed only in the crucible of pain. Pain teaches us who we really are, what we are really like, and what we should do and be. As Bly has reminded men, the path to adulthood often makes a major detour through Woundedville. But, it leads to the mature man, the resurrected ruler of the soul, the *'ish* kind of man.

The Meaning of *Ish*

The fifth Hebrew word that has much to say about what it means to be a man today is the word *'ish*. It is usually translated "man, mankind, or husband."[1] Holladay lists additional meanings: "those of higher rank, a ruler of lower rank, and man of God."[2] The usage of *'ish* speaks not only of man but also of God, especially where God is portrayed as the Husband of His people (Hosea). However, the most important element about *'ish* is its apparent reference to the adult male. *'Ish* is always in contrast to the Hebrew terms *yeled* (young man),

na'ar (youth), and *zaken* (old man), the latter to be studied in
the next chapter.[3] In other words, *'ish* is the adult male, the
male in his maturity, not the young man, the youthful warrior,
nor the gray-headed sage. *'Ish* is the mature man, the man who
has been resurrected from the wounds of life and has a new
perspective on the meaning of life and manhood because of
that pain. This man knows who he is and is known for his
attributes.

'Ish as the Attributal Male: One Known by His Attributes

The most common usage found in Scripture for *'ish* is that he
is the man *of something*. In other words, when *'ish* is used it
describes man characterized by some attribute. He is a man of
bravery (1 Samuel 4:9, 26:15), a man of good presence, "good
looking" (1 Samuel 16:18), a man of kindness (Proverbs 11:17),
a man of either smooth skin or hairy skin (Genesis 27:11). He
may be known by his understanding (Proverbs 17:27), his peace-
fulness (Psalm 37:37), or his trustworthiness (Exodus 18:21). The
term *'ish* also precedes references to a man's occupation, calling, or social position. He is listed as a man of the priesthood
(Leviticus 21:9) or a man of the king or prince (Exodus 2:14). He
is also called a man of war (Deuteronomy 2:14). *'Ish* is used
more often than any other term to convey the title "man of
God" (seventy-five times). In this regard, *'ish* is also used for
the man of the Spirit (1 Samuel 10:6, Hosea 9:7).

These references suggest that the mature man is the man
known by his attributes. He is also connected to himself. He
knows who he is and what his attributes are and how they define
him. In other words, he has stopped trying to be the man others
want him to be. This man has gotten in touch with who he is,
both positively and negatively, and has decided to stop living
his life exclusively through the eyes of someone else.

In a dysfunctional society this has primary importance
for men who were only "conductors" of others' feelings in
their families of origin. Psychologist John Friel observes the
dynamic in the "over-mothered, under-fathered" system that
betrays true development of adult maleness in sons:

Moms gave a powerful covert message to their son. The message was: "I am disappointed by males. I am disappointed by your father. I secretly hate men. Be my little spouse and make up for it. Become a sensitive little man to please Mommy, and you will make Mommy happy forever. But know that while you are pleasing me, I will despise you and fear you and hate you because you are male, while in the same breath I will seduce you into being the sensitive, gentle male I have always longed for. I love men and hate them. I fear them and desire them. I need you, but I need you under my thumb, where I secretly wish I could put all men."[4]

With this covert emotional dynamic going on, the young boy can never just "be," he must be the person his mother needs him to be in order for her to feel good and keep her emotional balance about men intact. However, as Friel correctly observes, the father, if he is on the premises, may be delivering another covert message. Here's the message from the husband of this woman:

"My son, I need you to run interference for me with Mom because her needs frighten and overwhelm me. I never learned to be comfortable with my vulnerability or the vulnerability of others, so I will leave it up to you to take care of this for me. You are so good at it. Besides I need to be out making a living. So stay by Mom, be her surrogate husband. Listen to her problems, become gentle and sensitive. Fill in those gaps. You will turn out okay. Trust me. Oh, wait, one other thing. Because you will become a sensitive male, I will not like you or respect you. I will fear you as I fear your mother. I will see you as 'wimpy' and I will secretly hold you in contempt. But son, it will work out. Trust me."[5]

The result is a son who is very confused about who he is. He has been so busy being the emotional conductor or communicator between warring partners that he has no time or opportunity to deal with who he is or wants to be. It usually takes much work (and pain) later in his life for him to see this perspective and find out who he really is.

The mature man is a man of *his* attributes, not the attributes of someone else's wants or needs. During the time of wounding, a man gets in touch with where his wounding has taken place, sorts it out, and arrives at some new insights about himself as a man. That's why true maturity requires a time of adversity.

Thus, these *'ish* attributes are not easily classified. They cover the gamut of human-male experience, feelings, and vocations. The attributes combine the mental, emotional, physical, sexual, and occupational aspects of a man. Therefore, I conclude that attribual man represents man in his integration, differentiation, individualization, and dedication.

Integration
Freud, writing from his Viennese male perspective after seeing mostly repressed Victorian women as his clients, asked the profound question, "What is it that women really want?" He never really answered the question. Some have suggested that women don't really know either! However, it is a good question. Another psychologist turned the question upon men and asked them what they really wanted in *themselves* as men. A better question, I believe, because we need to understand ourselves before trying to understand the opposite sex. Friel's findings disclose that men want seven things: (1) to feel more, (2) to befriend more, (3) to learn to love, (4) to find meaningful work, (5) to father significantly, (6) to be whole, and (7) to heal and reconcile.[6] These findings reveal a deep-seated desire in men to be more integrated within themselves or to find some new aspects of their personhood that allow them to live more fully. They want a wider range of possibilities than they are presently experiencing. Each man wants a greater unity to his life that allows him more freedom to feel, enjoy, praise, reconcile, and see meaning in his important relationships.

The current fiasco with Prince Charles and Lady Diana illustrates the narrow way both sexes look to have their fantasies fulfilled in the other. Charles needed a beautiful virgin princess in order to make him king and generate an heir. Diana needed a "handsome," dashing prince in royal uniform to complete her dream of marrying Prince Charming and having more financial security than most women in the world. They could then settle down, have children, and live happily ever after.

We all now know the real story. The fairy tale has turned horror story. Charles and Diana sat on the castle wall; Charles and Diana had a great fall; and all the Queen's consorts and all the Queen's fortunes could not put poor Charles and Diana back together again! Biographies on both sides have pointed out the dysfunctional nature of their respective backgrounds. Could either Charles or Diana ever be who they really are, without being molded and shaped by "royal expectations"? In my opinion both were sort of one-dimensional people looking for fulfillment in the other. Charles wanted a beautiful virgin to give him sons, but he got a woman who wanted to have fun. Diana wanted a handsome, wealthy prince, but she got a bore! Perhaps both need to grow up a little.

Personally, I identify with Charles. Even though I have tried to expand my range of experiences by taking classes or developing new hobbies like snow skiing, most of the time I still end up in the same old rut. But I do think I am maturing a little because I am learning to feel new things. My wounding experiences in the ministry have brought me into contact with a part of me that has been denied for years—my anger. I have realized I can slip into rage at the drop of a hat. My wife for the most part has been very supportive of my getting in touch with my feelings. I desire much more, though. I want to enjoy sunsets more, to connect better with my wife and kids, and to really learn to feel something in God's presence.

Differentiation

The word *'ish* is also used with reference to women in contexts of contrast. *'Ish* is the husband or man of a woman. This brings out the issue of differentiation that exists at this stop on the male experience. My personal view of a boy's developmental journey toward manhood rests primarily on the issue of differentiation. For a boy to become a man he must first break free from his mother and find his father. Having done this, he must then break free from his father in order to find himself. After finding himself he can then find and unite in marriage with a woman. However, the journey for most men more likely involves never breaking free of their mother and then still hoping to find themselves in a wife. The wife then becomes a second mother. A mother can never make a boy into a man, whether it be the first or the substitute mother. Sam Keen affirms the reality that as men we must at some point "say good-bye to Woman." He observes,

> We can't be comfortable in intimacy with women
> because we have never been comfortable in being distant
> from them. Most modern men have never learned the
> joy of solitude. We have failed to define our identity,
> our purpose, our raison d'etre apart from our relation-
> ship with Woman . . . and having sold our souls for
> her approval, we are ill at ease. To become a man, a son
> must first become a prodigal, leave home and travel solo
> into a far country . . . to love a woman we must first
> leave Woman behind.[7]

To do this means seeing the differences between men and women, between our world and the women's world. This begins with our mothers. I must recognize that I am not my mother, nor do I live in my mother's world. But I am also not my father, and do not live in my father's world. I am similar to my father in many ways, but I am also different. He is not me. Just recently it has really grabbed me how different my son is from me. He looks like me, he is very athletic as I was, but he is not me. I must allow him to be different from me and become his own man. I must allow him to differentiate.

For some men, differentiation may not be related to the

family of origin or to current family relationships. It may relate to those times when I feel I am being pushed into someone else's agenda, or being pressed to respond to another's dream for my life, or having to be someone I am not. It may relate to the kind of bosses, mentors, or pastors I have had in the past. It is so easy to think that the way they did it was the right way or the only way. At some point, I believe our careers and entire approaches to life need to be scrutinized to see if we are doing no more than trying to emulate someone we admire or doing the opposite of someone we despise. Until we reject both as "not being me," they hold a hellish power over our souls and we will never be the rulers of our own spirits.

Levinson calls this differentiation of maleness "detribalization," a term I personally love. It is so graphic. We are all tribalized by parents, teachers, pastors, churches, systems of thought, and friends. These all have their place, but they can become substitutes if not barriers to our own development. Only after our wounding experience can we begin to reappraise and reframe the disillusionment we've suffered. Only then can we critically evaluate our tribalization for both its strengths and weaknesses. Levinson clarifies this:

> As a man becomes more individuated and more oriented to the Self, a process of "detribalization" occurs. He becomes more critical of the tribe—the particular groups, institutions that have the greatest significance for him, the social matrix to which he is most attached. He is less dependent upon tribal rewards, more questioning of tribal values, more able to look at life from a universalistic perspective.[8]

One thing I am often criticized for as a professor is that I don't necessarily represent the party line of the school or the denomination. Even though I see no "party line" apart from a broad, evangelical doctrinal statement, I take the complaint as a compliment. I have never intentionally tried to "detribalize," but I do value the critical role of thinking deeply about theological issues in light of our very pagan society. It is so easy merely to mouth what some other respected scholar said, or recite our particular tradition, rather than doing the hard work of thinking for oneself on the basis of Scripture. A mature man is one who can do the differentiation, but who often gives the appearance of being an individualist.

Individualization

To become a mature man requires not only differentiation, or knowing what one isn't, but also a certain individualization, learning what one *is*. Early in my career I was asked by a psychologist who reviewed each job applicant the earth-shattering question, "Who is Bob Hicks?" It shook me to the core because I couldn't remember anyone ever asking me the question before. I can't even remember what I answered. I'm sure I struggled around for some answer to cover my complete agnosticism. At the time all I knew was that I was a jock who had just graduated from college and become a Christian. That was it.

A few years ago a male counselor I was seeing asked the same question. Coming out of a time of real woundedness, all I could get out was my name, "Bob Hicks." He looked at me and asked, "Is that it?" I looked him in the eye and said, "That's right, that's who I am!" I then added, "Are you going to sit there and tell me I'm not?" Then both of us broke out laughing. Since neither of us had been bestowed with the supernatural gift of total omniscience, neither of us could ever know whether or not there was more to the package. Personally, I think it's a bad question and therefore demands a bad answer. (That's the warrior in me still alive and well.) Of course, there is always much more to our being than we will ever know. If the counselor was asking for the kind of man I was, I could do better on that question since it gets at some of the personal attribute issues dealt with in this chapter. But finally, he looked at me and said, "I respect your courage to hold your ground on this question."

To answer "Who is Bob Hicks?" says many things and says nothing at all, for who really knows who this person is?

Only God knows me perfectly, for even my self-knowledge is distorted. As La Rochefoucauld so disturbingly said, "Our virtues are most frequently but vices in disguise."[9] It's hard to truly know oneself. Sometimes a spouse does a better job. After almost twenty-five years of marriage my wife says what bothers her most is my aloofness and living in my head. She's right, I must distance and separate at times in order to find the emotional and creative energy I need. Until I read Levinson's book about the stages in a man's life, I thought my distancing was sick. Now I see this is an essential requirement for men to survive the midlife transition period; but it can also be taken to extremes. Levinson cautions,

> Separateness fosters individual growth and creative adaptation, though it can be harmful when carried to an extreme . . . persons of all ages and occupations must deal with the Attachment/Separateness polarity. If we become too separate, our contact with the world is lost and our capacity for survival jeopardized. If we become too attached to the environment, we endanger our capacity for self-renewal, growth and creative effort. Although a balance of attachment and separateness must be found at every age, it will necessarily change from one era of the life cycle to the next. . . . In early adulthood the balance ordinarily shifts markedly toward attachment at the expense of separateness. During the twenties and thirties, a man is tremendously involved in entering the adult world and doing his work for the tribe. . . . During the Mid-life Transition, to do the work of reappraisal and de-illusionment, he must turn inward. He has to discover what his turmoil is about, and where he hurts. He wants to find and lick his wounds. Having been overly engaged in his worldly struggles, he needs to become more engaged with himself.[10]

Having been engaged with himself, a man is in a much better position to know how he feels about a lot of things.

He knows what he wants to be and do and what he does not want to be and do. He is becoming his own man, a prerequisite for maturity. From his time in the womb of the wound, he can emerge with a new vision for his life, a vision that is probably more realistic than the one he had in his warrior stage. The warrior doesn't factor in failure or weigh the ethics of warfare, he just fights. But men who have grown through their woundedness, and learned the critical issues that only woundedness can teach, have a more mature vision and dedication.

Dedication

The saddest men I know are the men who have no real vision for their lives. The man who goes to work every day, comes home, reads the paper, has dinner, watches television, and goes to bed—only to repeat the pattern the next day—is not alive or well. Life has been reduced to mere functioning and maintaining.

Even as I write these words, fear grips my heart, because I know this is how I often feel that I am perceived by my own wife and children. Do they know what it is that drives me, that makes me want to get up in the morning? Are they aware of what makes me want to stay alive and hang in there during this span of years called life? Though my life may be clear to me (a big assumption), I fear it still may not be clear to the ones I love. But to be truly alive a man needs a vision, a meaning for his life.

Remember what psychologist Friel said men (even secular men) want? They want to see meaning in the work they do. They are tired of merely providing without seeing a larger purpose than paying bills. A bumper sticker sums up the perspective: "Every damn day the same as before." As warriors, we are filled with dreams. We are Prince Charles looking for our Diana. But then we get wounded, bored, and frustrated. We finally conclude that life has no meaning, and the dream dies. On many days while I am teaching, disturbing questions break into my consciousness: "Why are you teaching this? . . . Do you really believe this? . . . Who are you to be saying that? . . . You don't really have anything to give, do you?" These questions, lingering from my wounding period, try to convince me to quit, change careers, and go get a real job. Almost at the same time another voice kicks in with, "You do have something to give! Minister out of your pain. You know the Scriptures—relate them to the lives of your students."

It is the mature, *'ish* kind of man who begins to rekindle the dream, modify the original vision, and return to the dedication lost in *Enosh* City (Woundedville). The *gibbor* is full of intense dreams—to win, to be right, to achieve, to be highly regarded—but with wounding these begin to fade. Yet with the reflection, integration, differentiation, and individualization that takes place following, a man can begin to have dreams again. Not necessarily with the same intensity, perspective, or urgent quality of the warrior stage, however. Now the dedication or rededication involves more insight. It requires the integration of larger and broader issues and is more related to the whole of life. As Levinson reveals, "It is no longer essential to succeed, no longer catastrophic to fail. He evaluates his success and failure in more complex terms, giving more emphasis to the quality of experience, to the intrinsic value of his work, and their meaning to himself and others."[11]

I have seen this change of perspective in my own life. When I graduated from seminary, I was ordained in a Baptist church and stood firmly in the baptistic tradition. But in my first pastorate, God brought across my path a Presbyterian minister who needed a place to hold services. His church started using our facility Sunday afternoons, and the pastor and I got to know each other. What came out of our dialogue and interaction was two years of breakfast meetings where we prayed and read Scripture together. Our spirits united, though our churches did not, and each of us was enriched by the other. Now those labels—Presbyterian and Baptist—don't have the same power or defining significance for me that they once had.

Some of my early "counselees" were individuals whom I

once thought were logical contradictions. God brought to me Christians who were homosexuals and Marxists. I listened, tried to understand, debated back and forth, but was left with the conviction that they were sincere about both their faith in Christ and their views on sexuality and politics, though these views differed from mine. I have problems maintaining a view of sexuality or politics that is incompatible with clear biblical injunctions (against homosexual behavior) or clear biblical teaching on human nature (which is contrary to Marxism's "new man"). My last visit to the Air Force Chaplain School also broke down some long-standing categories. At the beginning of the school, a Catholic priest gave one of the most heartfelt testimonies about what God was doing in his life and how much he wanted our time at the school to be a time of reflection on God and our walk with Him. He concluded by saying, "I want you to be born again here as I have been." Oh, don't get me wrong, I haven't become Catholic, or a Marxist, or gay. I don't condone Marxist politics or homosexual behavior. But I have learned that the way to look at God or the world is not necessarily through the lens or categories I currently believe are the correct ones. The labels don't matter all that much, whether they be Communist, Democrat, New Age, feminist, fundamentalist, or hookers-married-to-cross-dressing codependents.

I think I now see the world and people differently because I try to look beyond the labels to the person, his unique situation, station, and needs. I fail often and get hooked back into my old warrior responses, but now I consciously recognize that pattern for what it is. I believe this is the way Jesus related to people, and His modeling provides me with a much richer and broader perspective on ministry.

My vision for ministry is still the same but different. I hold the same commitments I had in my twenties, but I hold them differently, some more firmly, others with less significance. My warrior used to see all theological issues the same and equal. I defended them all with the same swing of the sword. Now I swing less often, but when I do, look out! You have challenged me at the heart of my dedication.

Elton Trueblood said, "Men cannot live well either in poverty or in abundance unless they see some meaning and purpose in life, which alone can be thrilling. Lacking the joy which comes from meaning and purpose, we turn to all kinds of wretched substitutes."[12] I see men today being committed to the stock market, football games, and individual pastimes only because no one has ever challenged them to higher purposes. Of course, this is individual. Part of being an *'ish* man is the individualizing of the calling and mission. But I do need a mission that has very little to do with my profession, station, or marital status. John Henry Newman, the founder of the Oxford Movement, having been rejected by both the Anglican Church from which he had come and the Catholic Church to which he was converting, wrote:

> God has created me, to do Him some definite service;
> He has committed some work to me which He has not
> committed to another. I have my mission—I may never
> realize it in this life, but I shall be told in the next. I am
> a link in a chain, a bond of connection between persons.
> He has not created me for nothing. I shall do good, I
> shall do His work. Therefore, I will trust Him. Whatever,
> wherever I am. I cannot be thrown away.[13]

I see this statement as a rich example of an *'ish* kind of man struggling to make his life count for something, though he did not know exactly the shape it might take.

By getting in touch with who we are and doing the necessary reappraisal of our attributes, we are in a better position to continue our growth more wholistically. The warrior is in reality a one-dimensional man, focused on his gun; the phallic male is, of course, over focused on his penis; while the wounded male cannot see beyond his own hurt. Therefore, with the mature man there begins a new symmetry to life, a new depth and richness not experienced before. But this wholistic advancement does not mean the man has become an isolated individual apart from the people he cares about. Attributal man is also a newly emerging relational man.

Ish as Relational Man
One of my criticisms of the current state of counseling is that the proposed cure for codependent relationships is that the client must so individualize and differentiate from the dependent relationship that very little responsibility to the spouse is left intact. The entire focus is centered on "breaking free" in order to become a more whole person. I agree this must take place to some degree in order to have healthy relationships, but at the same time, I don't think true marital health is achieved merely by having two totally separate, well-differentiated people in the relationship. What this amounts to is two individuals doing their own thing and going their own separate ways. In fact, "becoming self-actualized"—whatever that is supposed to mean—may be nothing more than a cover for selfishness. A Christian view of marriage or any significant relationship must maintain the element of responsibility to one another to be truly Christian. We *are* our brothers' and sisters' keepers. But today this language has been condemned as the language of codependent relationships. People in biblical relationships always have some feeling of being responsible for another human being and wanting to maintain connection with that person. This is precisely what is seen in other uses of *'ish*.

'Ish is commonly used with a similar-sounding word, the word for woman, *ishah*. It's first seen in Genesis 2:23, where Adam names his wife with a name that is his own name (*ish*), only with an added feminine ending. This may reflect the subtle statement that she is like him (human) and not like the animals. Likewise, looking at her newly fashioned birthday suit, Adam realizes there are also significant differences. She is like him but not like him. Several commentators suggest that this "naming" establishes the marriage relationship as a relation of equals. She is not an animal to be lorded over, and he is not a wimp without the authority to name her.[14]

With the mature man I believe this idea of equality has

a greater potential for realization. The warrior has relationships built around power, authority, and "chain of command." Being the lord of the home means being the commander of a unit or the drill sergeant. This is the paradigm upon which the warrior operates in his relationships, whether with his wife or children. For years I have used a marital enrichment tool called ENRICH. At one church I served, I did a study of one hundred couples from various age groups (newly marrieds, two to five years; middle marrieds, twenty to twenty-five years; and older marrieds, over thirty years). The most consistent pattern that emerged among all the groups was that intimacy or connection was always grounded in structure, order, and rules. This particular evangelical church approached Christian marriage with a teaching that was based more on rule-keeping and role-keeping than on the more intimate sharing of spirits. These marriages were more of the warrior type than marriages of mature men and women.

Phallic man can easily join with *'ishah* in sexual intercourse, but there is seldom any real joining of spirits. He is still trying to have his ultimate sexual fantasy fulfilled with the woman in his life. This makes her more an object than a person of equal stature. Several years ago author Marabel Morgan, in her best-selling *The Total Woman*, encouraged women to be the fantasy lover for their husbands. Whether it was having sex under the dining room table or dressing in Saran wrap and greeting him at the door, women were urged to appeal to the phallic natures of men. I read the book and really liked it. What real man wouldn't? But it represents a phallic approach to marriage.

The wounded male usually becomes impotent in his significant relationships. Whether with his kids or his wife, he isolates himself to lick his wounds and, like an animal, growls when anyone comes near. It's very difficult for women or anyone else to have a significant relationship with a wounded man.

Having said what I did about Marabel Morgan, I do want to clarify that the usages of *'ish* and *'ishah* do convey many strong sexual overtones to the marriage relationship. Passages such as Genesis 16:3, 19:8, 24:16, and Leviticus 15:16 all reveal that sexual activity and its regulation are very important aspects of *'ish*. From this perspective, we may conclude that only the mature man can experience a sexual relationship with his wife that is based on complete, unabashed union of spirits. This may be where the genuine fantasy sexuality so dreamed of by the phallic male actually finds fulfillment in a new, refreshing, creative sexuality. This apparently is what Solomon was encouraging in Proverbs 5:15-20. He blatantly tells his young listeners to seek their sexual outlet with the "*ishah* of their youth" and to become a man (*'ish*) satisfied and captivated by his wife's breasts only. That means we men have the joyous liberty of enjoying our wives for the glory of God. The desires of phallic men never end, but their focus can be realized by the mature male in his later years with the wife he committed himself to in his younger days.

After thirty-some years of marriage this stands to reason. We'd hope that both partners are no longer playing games; they know themselves and each other very well, and a new sexual freedom sets in. I have heard from older mentors that the best sex is yet to come. I can't wait!

'Ish is seen not only in marital relations but also in a man's national and communal relations. He is a man of friends (Proverbs 18:24); a man belonging to certain groups, whether to his tribe or nation (Numbers 25:6, Judges 10:1); and he is a man who holds a wide range of civic and social responsibilities. In Exodus 21–22, *'ish* will be found in all the domestic relations; in issues of harm to neighbors, family, and property; in treatment of servants; in what to do about stolen or destroyed property; and in crimes against people. In other words, the mature man is involved in civic responsibilities, carrying out the tough ethical and moral responsibilities that a fallen world creates. He is involved with friends, his culture, his tribe, and his nation. It is by these things that he is known and valued.

We live in an international economy today. Global politics dominate. I am even told that I have to be a "world Christian." I believe these things, but I also believe that to embrace them

I don't have to cease being who I am. I am also an American; a native midwesterner (Kansas); a male who likes good-looking southern women (I married one), Hawaiian beaches, Middle-Eastern food, Bach, Handel, Credence Clearwater Revival, Dire Straits, and Lamb. How do I put all that together as a Christian? I have no idea! But I know they are all a part of me; it's who I am. Take any one of them away and I have been robbed of some of my unique personhood. Just as 'ish was a man of Israel, a man of the tribe of Issachar, a man of friends, so am I a man of many things, the sum of which is who I am.

Being in the military and ministry has allowed me to see many other parts of the world. I would call myself a "world Christian" because I share the concerns of God for our world. Yet, I always feel a unique emotion when I return from overseas and enter the customs area at airports. A sign usually divides arriving passengers into non-U.S. citizens and U.S. citizens. My heart always leaps when I see the sign that says, "U.S. Citizens—Welcome Home." I enjoy ministry in foreign places. I like the people I meet and I think I could live in many other parts of the world, but America is my home. I will never apologize or be made to feel guilty about being an American. Maybe it's time we men thought more about what it *does* mean to be an American and what our responsibility is to our country. I don't believe this responsibility is in opposition to the concerns of the world or world missions, but it goes along with my local and national responsibilities. God and country are both important realities in my life. I don't ever want my country to be above God, but taking my relationship with God seriously does not negate my national or civic responsibilities. It does, in fact, require me to take those responsibilities seriously as well (Romans 13). Being a mature man is being a man of my church, my work, my community, my children's activities, and the things I just enjoy. To think like this, or to give myself the freedom to enjoy such things, means I am becoming a royal kind of person and taking back some rulership of my life.

Ish as Royal Man

While doing this study, I was struck by the way *'ish* is commonly used of God, the angel of the Lord, and men by the designation "man of God." Individuals of rank, priests, prophets, and those who bring messages from God are called *'ish elohim*, or man of God. This usage implies divine agency, empowering, and representation, if not divine rule through human means. In other words, what was lost in the Fall and through our woundedness begins to be recovered during the more mature stages of life. We were created to rule, but we lost the ability in the Fall. However, through redemption and the empowering work of the Spirit, a certain amount of recovery and new mastery is available to our lives (Galatians 5:1, Ephesians 5:1–6:17, Colossians 2:20-23). But the perspective gained from the paradigm created by these Hebrew words may imply that the reality of being a "man of God" comes much later than is usually taught. Although *'ish elohim* occurs seventy-five times in the Old Testament, and is used of Moses (Deuteronomy 33:1), Samuel (1 Samuel 9:6), David (Nehemiah 12:24), Elijah (1 Kings 17:18), and Elisha (2 Kings 4:7-13), ironically there is no similarity in the lives of these diverse men. In each case you'll see many godly things about their lives. But by what criteria was the term "man of God," the royal aspect of their divine King, applied to these men?

Perhaps this more simply raises the issue of whether a young man can really be a "man of God" in the sense of the royal man given in these passages. Perhaps to be declared as such takes some life blows, some disgraceful periods, while still faithfully trying to do what God has asked to be done. We are given some help as to what the royal man requirements are. They take time to develop.

When David was on his deathbed he had Solomon, his heir to the throne, brought to him. He then gave to his son his wisdom about being king and a man. He said, "I am about to go the way of all the earth. Be strong [a warrior], therefore, and show yourself a man [*ish*]" (1 Kings 2:2). Here we see the warrior element combining with the mature requirements of being king. From one father to one son, David shares how to be a good kind of ruler as a man. Basically, David tells Solomon he is going to need much strength to do what God requires him to do as a man. So prove yourself to be a man by doing these two things: Walk in the Lord's ways, and keep the law. Solomon's life was to be oriented around the Lord and, as king, to be the personal guardian and enforcer of the divine ordinances to the nation.

However, to do all this requires a particular obsession for a king. To rule with divine wisdom and integrity, the king cannot rule by the arbitrary whims of his own personality, but by the divine standards revealed in Scripture. This was made very clear in God's word to Moses before entering the Promised Land. God says,

> "When [a king] takes the throne of his kingdom, he is to write for himself on a scroll a copy of this law, taken from that of the priests, who are Levites. It is to be with him, and he is to read it all the days of his life so that he may learn to revere the LORD his God and follow carefully all the words of this law and these decrees and not consider himself better than his brothers and turn from the law to the right or to the left." (Deuteronomy 17:18-20, NIV)

The point is acutely clear: The king can rule only by obtaining, writing, reading, and making the Law (Torah) his personal obsession. He rules his life and his nation by means of the Word of God. The mature king, as well as the mature man, is one who rules his life with the wisdom of the Scriptures. What is required of the kings also turns out to be the "blessedness" of the mature man, who meditates on God's Word.

My first Hebrew research paper in seminary was not very encouraging. The assignment was to do a full "exegesis," or interpretation, of Psalm 1. I barely passed with a C-. The reason I didn't do very well on the paper was because I hadn't done enough homework on this very word, *'ish*. To my astute

Hebrew professor the meaning of this term was the key to the entire psalm. I had focused only on the relational and attribual aspects of the word and missed entirely the royal element. Therefore, he passed me by the grace of God. The point I had missed was that the blessing that accrues to *'ish* is that he no longer listens to the outside counsels of evil men, but only to the insights obtained through a diligent meditation on the Word of God. In other words, the way this *'ish* kind of mature man rules his life is by meditating and listening to voice of God in Scripture:

> Blessed is the man [*ish*] who does not walk in the
>   counsel of the wicked,
> Nor stand in the path of sinners,
> Nor sit in the seat of scoffers!
> But his delight is in the law of the LORD,
> And in His law he meditates day and night.
> (Psalm 1:1-2)

Because this psalm opens the Psalter, it may be the definitive statement about what the mature man looks like and how you and I may become one!

I believe this is the final individualization for *'ish*. I value the counsel I have received over the years from outsiders — both Christian and not-so-Christian. However, at some point each of us must realize that it is only I who will live my life. I must sort out all the potential consequences that could come to me based upon the decisions I make. I need this final individualization based on biblical statutes to occur so that neither Christians nor nonChristians can lead me astray. A real man must grow up in his relation to others, and this means growing up through the Scriptures and becoming less dependent upon pastors, professors, wives, churches, or parachurches. We need to be strong and prove ourselves to be men, by knowing and ruling our lives through deep scriptural insight.

Who is this *'ish* kind of man biblically? Surprisingly, we find the prophet Elijah at this point on the masculine journey.

Elijah: The Mature, Reborn Man

The Canaanites lived in an uneasy tension with the nation of Israel. They worshiped Baal, a nature and fertility deity. But after Israel's King Ahab took a pagan Canaanite wife, Jezebel, Israel's decline was no longer tolerable. God raised up the warrior Elijah to deal with the situation. God told him to leave home and go to the brook Cherith, across the Jordan. He immediately left and saw God feed and care for him miraculously (1 Kings 17:5-6). At a later date, God told him to go beyond Israel to Sidon to a certain widow of Zarephath. Elijah obediently complied, and again God worked miraculously in the supernatural multiplication of food and by raising the widow's son from the dead (17:7-24). Not a bad start for a young prophet. He does everything God tells him to do and, presto, God comes through, miraculously.

Having experienced success in these small ministries, Elijah is now ready for the big time, a larger church! God calls him to take on King Ahab and the prophets of Baal. The next scene is classic warrior stuff, attended by all the pomp, emotional conflict, and drama one could hope for. Elijah tells Ahab pointblank, "You have forsaken the commandments of the LORD, and have followed the Baals" (18:18). So Ahab summons all the prophets of Baal to take on this young, upstart warrior. Not to be outdone, Elijah challenges them to a contest: "Let's see who can call down fire from Heaven to consume two bulls." Heavy stuff! Way out on the limb now, in the name of God. But again, God comes through, bringing down the fire. Then, just as Elijah promised, God brought the rain to cure Israel's famine. The result was a glorious victory for Yahweh and Elijah. All the people declared, "The LORD, He is God; the LORD, He is God" (18:39).

Meanwhile, back at the office, Ahab returns from Carmel to find his adoring wife, Jezebel, anxiously awaiting every detail about what happened. Ahab sits down over a cup of coffee, shares every nugget, and she goes through the roof. Now we see the real power struggle shaping up. Feminists often blame all violence on Mafia patriarchy, but here the violent death threat is initiated and commanded by the matriarch (19:1-2)! She sends a messenger to Elijah to announce that a mafia-like hit has been planned against him.

The next verse says that Elijah "was afraid and arose and ran for his life" (19:3). Now, why would Elijah run? This prophet was not scared to leave his hometown, or to cross the Jordan, or to live without any provisions. He wasn't scared of the women in Sidon, or King Ahab, or the powerful prophets of Baal. So why Jezebel? The reader is not told, but we men can imagine it. Wouldn't we really rather stand up to our bosses, our fathers, Communists, atheists—anyone besides an irate, verbally threatening woman?

Apparently, Elijah did not sense God coming through for him this time. God does not tell him to flee to the desert, but he goes anyway, all the way to Beersheba. By the time he arrives, he is exhausted by both the trip and the events that led up to his disillusionment.

On the edge of the desert he pulls in and sleeps for days. He awakes, eats, and goes back to sleep. Typical wounded male behavior. The warrior is now hurting and bleeding, wounded by his lack of faith that God would take care of Jezebel, or by the fear of a death sentence on his life. In response, he asks God to take his life (19:4). I have uttered almost the exact words at times! Once refreshed he doesn't return to fight again; instead, he gets up and flees at least 60 to 150 more miles south (depending upon where one places Mount Horeb in Sinai) and takes up residence in a cave. In other words, Elijah is now as far from the ministry and his vocation as he can get. I have been there mentally as well several times! As Howard Hendricks has said, "If I knew where to turn in my prophet's badge, I would."

During this time of woundedness God begins to deal with Elijah and turn him toward becoming a mature prophet and an *'ish* kind of man. Anyone who has stood on the edge of the Sinai realizes this is truly a wilderness. But in the Scriptures it represents a place not only of testing but also of tutoring. It is here that God asks the all-important question, "What are you doing here, Elijah?" (19:9). Elijah's answer *almost* rings true: "I have been very zealous for you, because the Israelites have rejected you, but I alone have been faithful." It is true that he had been zealous; it is *not true* that only Elijah was faithful. Later God will inform him that there are still seven thousand who haven't caved in to Baal (19:18).

Next, God adds some brilliant fireworks, special effects of truly biblical proportions! Hurricane-force winds blow through the desert, but God does not allow Himself to be seen in them. Then an earthquake and a fire, but likewise, the Lord is not perceived in these either. Then comes the gentle whisper of God, which Elijah does hear (19:13). He moves to the doorway of the cave (his first outward movement) and hears God say again, "What are you doing here, Elijah?" Elijah answers with the same response about doing God's work and being the only faithful one. Then God gives him a new vision for his life, telling him to go back, anoint a new king, and anoint a new prophet to succeed him (19:15-16)! "Oh, and by the way, Elijah," God says, "I have seven thousand other faithful that you don't know about."

What has happened here? We have seen the maturing of a man. Elijah, the classic warrior, enjoys success and victory in doing God's work. All is well, as long as God comes through the way Elijah expects Him to come through. But finally, the power of a woman over his life throws him for quite a loop. He flees into woundedness to nurse the hurt, fear, and depression. He wants nothing more to do with his vocation, his relationships, or his nation. He becomes so self-absorbed that he barely tastes food and does only the minimal requirements for living.

Here the voice of God comes to him, not in the spectacular fireworks he had become familiar with, but in the stillness and silence. The voice of God then begins to renew the vision for Elijah's life. It is the same calling but a different vision. God allows Elijah to reconnect with his prophetic mission yet now see it differently. His new ministry will not be anointed and invested with divine fireworks as before, but the anointing and investing of his life will be in others, even his replacement. Now he no longer has to jump to Ahab's challenges or run from Jezebel's threats. He is a mature man, a man now capable of ruling his own soul because he has been wounded and has recovered through hearing the word of God in a refreshingly different way. A man thus reborn and resurrected is then ready to be the mentor and sage to a younger man.

Levinson concludes,

> When a man no longer feels that he must be a remarkable writer, craftsman or leader, he is more free to be himself and to work according to his own wishes and talents. The chances are that he will contribute more to society when his life contributes more to and expresses more of his self.[15]

As a mature man, Elijah is now free to fail and free to give more of himself to others. He is free to take on Ahab and Jezebel without having so much on the line. He is free to became a sage and pour his remaining years into his protégé, Elisha.

For us, this is where we gain understanding and hope: that the *'ish* kind of man can pull out of his woundedness and take the road less traveled. Robert Frost says this road may be less traveled, but he knows at a certain point of his adult life he cannot proceed along the more-traveled *and* the less-traveled way, so he ponders both of them. Frost is insightful because he realizes that one road eventually leads to another and in taking one he will never realistically make it back to explore the other. My dear brother readers, I believe this stage of the masculine journey is an important crossroads for us. We can go one way or another, but not both. It's time to look back and ponder whether we have just taken the road most traveled, the one of less difficulty but more popularity. It may have been the right road for you. But are you still wondering about the other road? Consider taking it. Count the cost of taking it. Think about the kind of life you want in the years ahead. Make your decision and move on. What a difference it will make at the next stop. Frost gives his vision poetic form:

> Two roads diverged in a yellow wood,
> And sorry I could not travel both
> And be one traveler, long I stood
> And looked down one as far as I could
> To where it bent in the undergrowth;
>
> Then took the other, as just as fair,
> And having perhaps the better claim,
> Because it was grassy and wanted wear;
> Though as for that, the passing there
> Had worn them really about the same,
>
> And both that morning equally lay
> In leaves no step had trodden black.
> Oh, I kept the first for another day!
> Yet knowing how way leads on to way,
> I doubted if I should ever come back.
>
> I shall be telling this with a sigh
> Somewhere ages and ages hence:
> Two roads diverged in a wood, and I—
> I took the one less traveled by,
> And that has made all the difference.[16]

CHAPTER SEVEN

The Sage —
Zaken: The Fulfilled Man

◆

Delighted to be but wise,
For men improve with the years.

WILLIAM BUTLER YEATS
"Men Improve with the Years"

Give me a young man in whom there is something
of the old, and an old man with something
of the young; guided so,
a man may grow old in body, but never in mind.

CICERO
De Senectute, XI

IT'S HARD TO beat Middle-Eastern hospitality. Rooted in the centuries-old Bedouin traditions where passing caravans would erect tents in the desert, roast lamb, mix their *hummus* (beans), and break bread together for hours, there's nothing like it anywhere else in our world today. For those who travel in that part of world, the millennia-old customs can still be seen and experienced. The tent is the place where the elder men of the tribes gather in the afternoon heat to sip tea and do "majlis" administration.[1] As understood by this Westerner, this is where the elders gather on soft pillows, drink tea, and discuss the affairs of the day. Also at this time anyone from any tribe can come and air his complaints to the elders, as well as ask for advice on any matter. Tea or coffee is served to visitors, and everyone reclines or sits. This rich event may appear to us as just "shooting the breeze," but it is an interesting mix of social hospitality, business wheeling and dealing, personal counsel, and administrative justice. I have seen this "tent fellowship" only from a distance at the edge of the Sinai. The most common feature I noticed from my vantage point was the white-robed, gray-haired, bearded men gathered in circles, drinking their tea, and speaking with great intensity as illustrated by their hand gestures. These were elders, doing what elders do.

This concept plays itself out in a radically different way in American church life. When I think of the elders gathered together in most of the churches I have served, it hardly resembles anything close to what I saw in the desert. In our typical elder meetings there is very little true hospitality (usually only coffee), and we sit around a table made more for business board meetings. Rather than the random, relational approach of the Bedouins' tent meeting, we have an agenda, minutes, and Robert's Rules of Order. When I look around the room, few of the men have beards, or even gray hair. Most are white-collar executives still very much in their warrior stage of manhood. With a few exceptions, most of these elder meetings could pass for board meetings at General Motors, except that we open with prayer and have a devotional.

As I compare these two images of elders, I obviously feel more compatible with the Middle-Eastern motif. I'll take the pillows, reclining, *hummus*, and pita, with Arab coffee and tea any day. This is where the young come to learn about business, marriage, sex, politics, and how to get the most mileage out of a camel. The gray-headed, bearded elder was a man in his prime, a man with the wisdom of life. At least that was the expectation. These were the wise men the society looked to as their leaders and mentors. To be an elder some day was the chief aspiration of young men. These men were old but not retired. They were involved, nurturing, leading, modeling, and contributing.

Today, rather than gathering in tents, our seniors are found huddled in retirement enclaves separated from the mainstream of society and the young. They play golf, bridge, and tennis, watch reruns, and wait for their kids to call. They live in "adult" communities, "life care" facilities, and "senior-citizen" villages. Such nicely coined marketing phrases cover up the reality that they are almost completely cut off from the rest of the community. When they get together in community centers, it is with their own kind.

I know I have overstated the contrast between these two senior-citizen groups. It's always easy to criticize where you are not! Since God has a profound sense of humor, I will probably end up in a retirement home sooner than I think! But right now, it's the last place I want to be.

For our last stop on the masculine journey, I will try to portray how I believe the Scriptures ideally conceive this last stage of life. At the front end, let me say very frankly, the biblical sage, or *zaken*, has far more in common with the aforementioned Bedouin elder than with anything we currently see in American life.

Zaken: A Word Study of the Gray-Headed Man

As alluded to in the Bedouin elder, this final Hebrew word for man, *zaken*, has as its primary meaning, "beard." The verbal idea carries the connotation of "being old or becoming old." In Arabic the word is used of a "camel with its lower lip hanging down."[2] That's old! Holladay summarizes the meaning as, "the totality of men with full beard of mature years with legal competence in the community."[3] By contrast, our culture sees the senior citizen as barely having any competence at all.[4]

The word *zaken* is often contrasted to the young man (*na'ar*). In a very striking passage God tells the nation of Israel that if they don't obey Him, He will bring a foreign nation upon them who will have no respect for the *zaken* or pity for the young (*na'ar*).

Zaken is also found in close proximity with its synonym *seb*, which means "to be gray or old."[5] Thus, Samuel is "old and gray" (1 Samuel 12:2), as is Abraham (Genesis 15:15). Throughout the Old Testament the *zaken* also represents various social groups: cities (Deuteronomy 19:12), regions (Judges

11:5-11), tribes (1 Samuel 30:26), or nations (Numbers 11). This elder then is far removed from our modern concepts of the retired, uninvolved senior citizen. Instead, his focus is on the social community to which he belongs, either holding office or representing the various groups he values.

As I was working on this chapter, I took a break to go to Holly's, a local hangout—part bar, part restaurant, and part grocery store. Its outside deck overlooks the coming together of the Blue Ridge Mountains and Grandfather Mountain. It offers quite a spectacular view on a clear day. That day the deck hosted a family from Poland, a romantic college couple (who couldn't keep their hands off each other), and me. The romantic couple was oblivious to both the view and the rest of us. They were both very phallic! However, the family from Poland entertained me with a great story, and I felt we got to know one another a bit. But this young couple in their early twenties did not know or care that the rest of us existed, even though this Polish family told a fascinating tale about their narrow escape from death and imprisonment during the Communist years. After all, this is modern America, where the old and gray are written off as having nothing to contribute to the young and beautiful.

I suppose I don't blame them. I'm sure that's exactly how I felt when I was twenty, and that girl was far better looking than most of the girls I dated (with the exception of my wife). But today, most twenty-year-olds look at people in their thirties as "over the hill." When one is thirty years old, forty is a real threat, and fifty-year-olds seem ready for the nursing home. That's how far our current culture is from most of the ancient cultures. I realize we cannot return to the days of yore, but it helps to see the contrast between our current youth-worshiping culture and the biblical perspective that values older adults.

So what do the Scriptures tell us about the *zaken*, this sage of ancient societies? Fundamentally, this stop on the masculine journey is the goal of manhood, the place of genuine fulfillment, and—this may come as a real shock—the time of most significant contribution.

Zaken as the Goal of Manhood

One modern tragedy affecting men is that they are burning out at such alarming rates. They are in such a hurry to get wherever they are headed. As an old country preacher said, they are "hurryin' big for little reasons." If our goal of being a man is to be the CEO, or to make our first million, or to have our dream home at the lake, or to pastor a large church by the time we are forty, then we have every reason to be "hurryin' big." Time is running out and we are not there yet. Sometimes women contribute to this view. They see other men providing these things for their wives, so they think that is normative. I doubt if such productivity really is all that normative in our culture, but even if it is, such a race is not normative by biblical standards. The Scriptures provide us with a much longer look at this thing called manhood. At forty, we are just kids!

At the end of Moses' life, he wrote a song to teach the nation of Israel to remember what God had done for them:

> Remember the days of old,
> Consider the years of all generations.
> Ask your father, and he will inform you,
> Your elders [zakenim], and they will tell you.
> (Deuteronomy 32:7)

In other words, when one generation is on the verge of denying the ability of God to do something, bring in the elders! They have the knowledge, history, and experience with God to know what really happened, how God works, and how you should trust Him today. The psalmist says the same thing: "I have been young, and now I am old [zaken]; yet I have not seen the righteous forsaken" (Psalm 37:25).

Oh, how I need to know this! There have been so many times in my life where I would debate this truth. I would say, "Wait a minute, I know people who are righteous but who have starved to death." That's when the insight of the zaken is needed to ask, "Yes, but were they forsaken?" Maybe they are singing praise to God at this very moment! Without the experience and perspective of the *zaken*, we are left to look at life from a limited vantage point.

Therefore, we need to see the goal of manhood as becoming a wise, experienced elder of our generation. This has more to do with what we have learned from life than what we have accomplished in our warrior and our *ish* mature years. The goal is to be a gray-headed old man who has some wisdom to pass on to the next generation.

Not long ago I went through a period where I was consciously resisting this goal. My wife, Cinny, looked at me one day and said, "Your hair is really getting gray; why don't you put something on it?" Why do we call it *"pre*mature" gray, anyway? Gray might signal true maturity with nothing "pre" about it! Anyway, I went out and bought some Grecian Formula. I fought the battle for about a year. My mother didn't like it, my secretary didn't like it, and finally Cinny said she liked it better the other way. Then my own pride set in. I was the only one who "liked" my hair without the gray. I realized I was trying to hang on to my vanishing youth. I could use my wife as justification, but the real reason I did not like being gray was that I didn't like being perceived as "older." In researching this book, my study of *zaken* reminded me that there is real dignity and honor to the gray head (Proverbs 16:31, 20:29). A balding friend also told me, "Just be thankful you have hair to be gray."

I threw out my Grecian Formula and faced the fact I am getting older. Now I hope to have the silver-gray hair my father-in-law had. It was beautiful. The gray head is not something to hide but to value, because it is the goal of manhood. We really should be pitying the young men with their full heads of dark, thick hair. They lack such wisdom!

If gray-headedness is the embodiment of lengthy life experience, something to be sought out by the younger generation, then this should be the goal and pursuit of all men. Of course, just because one has obtained a certain age or a head of silver hair does not mean he is wise. Both the psalmist and Elihu (in the book of Job) confirm the reality that age does not

necessarily produce wisdom. The psalmist declares, "I understand more than the aged [*zakenim*], because I have observed
Thy precepts" (Psalm 119:100). In other words, wisdom comes
only from an obedient life before God. In this we find a unique
wisdom that age by itself cannot impart. Elihu, in trying to
defend Job in front of his other miserable counselors, says,

> I am young in years,
>   and you are old [*zaken*];
> that is why I was fearful,
>   not daring to tell you what I know.
> I thought, "Age should speak;
>   advanced years should teach wisdom."
> But it is the spirit in a man,
>   the breath of the Almighty, that gives him under-
>   standing.
> It is not only the old who are wise,
>   not only the aged who understand what is right.
>   (Job 32:6-9, NIV)

Wisdom then is not a prerogative of age but of scriptural
insight and obedience. But this is only part of the goal. To be
a "wise" elder one must be doing some things when young to
ensure that wisdom is gained. Study of the Scriptures, faith
in God, trust in Christ, and obedience to biblical truth are all
part of the journey to ensure this fullness of manhood later
in life. Without these, the elderly life can be empty, dry,
and uninteresting. My greatest fear is becoming a dirty old
man. I can't prevent becoming an old man. But I can prevent
becoming a *dirty* old man! The physical and psychological
limitations noted in the Scriptures and medical textbooks are
fairly certain in their probability. Hence, 90-year-old Sarah
was certainly beyond the years of childbearing, and 100-year-
old Abraham apparently could no longer have an erection to
make pregnancy possible (Genesis 18:11-12). Solomon uses
this knowledge of the physical and psychological decline to
call on us to get on with our lives and do what we need to do

before the days of infirmity come upon us (Ecclesiastes 12:1-7).
Good advice!

Even though we no longer live in a culture that honors
the gray head or the senior citizen (besides giving them some
discounts), it is encouraging to note the biblical perspective
on aging. If followed, this one category of biblical admonition
could radically change our culture and the treatment of parents, grandparents, and seniors in the United States. Respect
and honor for the elder is rooted in the Ten Commandments,
where God says, "Honor your father and your mother, so that
you may live long in the land" (Exodus 20:12, NIV; emphasis
added). This is an interesting concept. As we give respect to
our older parents, we ensure a greater longevity for ourselves.
Or turning it around, if you don't want to live long, just treat
your parents with animosity!

God also revealed as a part of the Law of Israel that the
younger (whoever that is) should "rise in the presence of the
aged, show respect for the elderly and revere your God. I am
the LORD" (Leviticus 19:32, NIV). I always thought this was
some custom from the Deep South till I read this. It has changed
my whole perspective. Now I get up out of my seat when someone older enters the room. This is something to think about,
regardless of the culture we are in or how old we are! Proverbs
also records, "Listen to your father, who begot you, and do not
despise your mother when she is old" (23:22).

Hence, the goal of a man's life is to be a man of wisdom
late in life. This is an honorable station, one that should be
respected by the younger men, even though they may not
respond to it positively. If this honor has not come to our
elderly, it is not necessarily their fault. Those of us who are
younger must still lack the proper regard for them. *Zaken* is
the last stop on the male journey, the goal of manhood, the
time of genuine fulfillment. Go for it!

Zaken as the Time of Genuine Fulfillment

I am convinced most Americans (even Christians!) look for
fulfillment in all the wrong places and at all the wrong times.

Just as our hurried lifestyles rob us of the longer perspective on anything, so also the expectations we create for ourselves rob us of ever being fulfilled by anything. Consequently, we are constantly sacrificing the good of the present for the might-bes and wannabes in the future. As a result, we are rarely satisfied.

When I do retreats—whether with couples, singles, or men—I like to ask, "How many thoroughly contented people have you known?" Most can't think of any. For the few who do answer they usually mention a grandmother or someone older. It would seem that in a culture driven by advertising promises and the American Dream, we might find *some* satisfaction. I contend we are looking in the wrong places for it, and at the wrong time. Ultimately God has to be the source of our satisfaction. Jesus said it well: Only those who hunger and thirst for righteousness (which comes from God) will ever find it and be satisfied (Matthew 5:6). Beyond this, I believe we also look for it at the wrong time. We are looking for far more than our current lives can possibly give us.

While I was sitting in a restaurant one holiday, an attractive young lady came in wearing a Christmas sweatshirt. Across the front was inscribed in red printing: "Dear Santa, I want it all." In Western cultures, that's not considered too high of an expectation. Yet, most of the people I know are just surviving. Whether Christian, agnostic, atheist, or uncommitted, we are all in the same boat when it comes to unfulfilled expectations. I see Christians just as frustrated for not being able to pull off the American Dream as anyone else. Whether one has mortgage payments, business loans, kids in college, or other responsibilities to meet, I wonder if anyone has any sense of fulfillment. Perhaps the time of genuine fulfillment is far ahead of where we think it should be. If we would view the prime of life as age seventy rather than forty, suddenly the whole paradigm would change. We can relax, enjoy, celebrate, even tolerate the lack of fulfillment we may currently feel. My gut tells me we have just too many requirements, expectations, bills, phone calls, superficial acquaintances, meetings, teacher conferences, report cards, job evaluations, and financial cut-backs to find genuine fulfillment in anything.

What then brings this sense of fulfillment in the *zaken* stage of life? Most of us don't think about how we want to die. We live in a death-denying culture. Anything about death is spoken behind closed doors or in hushed tones. We quickly whisk the dead out of sight and commit them to hospitals, funeral parlors, and cemeteries. Most families performed these duties themselves in times past. When a person has to actually handle, dress, and bury a dead loved one, the whole perspective about death changes. So we don't think about it until we literally have to. But we should.

I must admit that before doing the study for this chapter, I had never really thought about how I wanted to die. Cinny and I have talked about where we would like to be buried, but that is about it. But how we would like to die is a completely different issue, an issue far more complex and subjective.

From the biblical perspective, the *zaken* stage is the time for ultimate fulfillment, wherein lies the satisfaction of living life fully to the very end. Accordingly, the real fulfillment lies in going to a natural death with our business taken care of and our important relationships reconciled. God said to Abraham, "You shall go to your fathers in peace; you shall be buried at a good old age" (Genesis 15:15). Even though the only piece of real estate Abraham ever owned was his wife's grave, the text says he lived 175 years, "breathed his last and died at a good old age, an old man and full of years" (25:8, NIV). Now that's something to put on your tombstone! The implication from the fullness of years is that Abraham lived right down to the wire. His long years allowed him to see the fullness of life. This may have been what was in the mind of the psalmist when he wrote,

> The righteous will flourish like a palm tree, . . .
>> planted in the house of the LORD,
>> they will flourish in the courts of our God.
> They will still bear fruit in old [*zaken*] age,

they will stay fresh and green,
proclaiming, "The LORD is upright;
   he is my Rock." (Psalm 92:12-15, NIV)

Solomon calls the crown of the righteous this gray-headed station of life: "Gray hair is a crown of splendor; it is attained by a righteous life" (Proverbs 16:31). This is of course the ideal.

One summer during my college years I had the opportunity to work in a hospital. I was a premed major and I wanted to see if I would get sick at the sight of blood! I passed that test, but I got a thorough education in many other areas. One was in the geriatrics ward. Every week all of the medical students and premeds would look at the board where our assignments were posted for the week. Everyone loved pediatrics and maternity. These were the fun wards. For the most part, everyone there is happy, kids are the best patients, and the atmosphere is always light and pleasant. However, the absolute worst and most dreaded ward was geriatrics. When you saw your name posted to that ward, you knew you were in for a very stress-filled week. Why was this ward reputedly the worst? Was it because no one likes having to watch men and women in their later years die? No, it is not just watching someone die, but watching *how* they die. There were some delightful exceptions. But for the most part, these dying people were cantankerous, bitter, demanding, and loaded down with regrets about almost everything.

What an education for this twenty-one-year-old that summer. Its imprint is still in my mind. I don't want to die that way. If this is the purportedly most-fulfilling stage of life, then where was the fulfillment? Certainly, the bitter spirits and regret can't be blamed totally on the physical ailments and diseases the patients were facing. The delightful exceptions had the same physical difficulties, if not worse ones. So how does one explain the difference? I couldn't then, but now I have a better perspective from which to evaluate it.

The Scriptures list three conditions that make the *zaken* time of life less than fulfilling. The first has to do with having no *zakens* in the family line. Eli's two sons wanted nothing to do with God. They had intercourse with their girlfriends on the very doorsteps of their place of worship, but were not disciplined by Eli (1 Samuel 2:22). Consequently, God sent a messenger to Eli to inform him that, because of his failures as a parent (he still gave his sons the best part of the sacrificial offerings), no man in his family would ever see the *zaken* stage of life. In other words, all relatives in the family of Eli, except Samuel, who had been dedicated to the Lord, would have shortened longevity. Now, I'm not proposing that this is an absolute principle today, whereby anyone who has no living relatives is under a curse from God. But it does say profound things about what makes life in our later years fulfilling: It is having family members around to age with. Whether they be siblings, cousins, nieces or nephews, aunts or uncles, relationships with extended family members are important ingredients to aging well.

A second cause for the lack of fulfillment during this stop on the map is recognizing the needless loss of life due to unnatural causes. There is something built into the rhythm of life that makes death a very natural thing. But when a life close to us is lost to unnatural causes, a part of us also dies. This seems inappropriate, unnatural, and unjust. That's why the losses of children and babies are often the hardest to deal with, even for the most experienced hospital personnel. There is a violation that has taken place in these deaths. One so young should not have to die.

My most difficult pastoral care has been with the parents of children who have died accidentally when life seemed to be only fine and good. When King David was on his deathbed, he alluded to the unnatural deaths that Joab, his own general, had engineered to get rid of two of his commanders. He tells his son Solomon that Joab "shed the blood of war in peace. And he put the blood of war on his belt about his waist, and on his sandals on his feet" (1 Kings 2:5-6). David, his life almost over, still felt badly about this event, and he made Solomon promise to avenge the injustice in order to make his passing a little less painful. Here the failures suffered under David's administration are on his mind as he is dying. Having this insight should teach us to take care of these things before we reach this stage of life so we can go to our graves with clear consciences.

The third detriment to fulfillment is suffering the loss of younger children. When the sons of Jacob came back from Egypt having not recognized their own brother Joseph as prime minister, they requested from their father that Benjamin, the youngest, be returned to Joseph. However, the pain of losing yet another son, his youngest to boot, was too great for the old man. He says, "My son shall not go down with you. . . . If harm should befall him on the journey you are taking, then you will bring my gray hair down to Sheol in sorrow" (Genesis 42:38). The gray-headed man does not want to go to his grave knowing that his own sons have preceded him in death. This robs a man of the joy of old age. On the other hand, the crown or reward of life for the *zaken* is seeing one's grandchildren (Proverbs 17:6).

What these obstacles to fulfillment have in common is the loss of life and of family connection. These become much more critical issues as one gets older. It goes beyond financial concerns and who will take care of us in our later years. These are commonly addressed by financial planners. But what this gets at is our own ability to suffer loss and move on from it. When you're old there are few places left to go.

A recent TV program reported the conclusions of the first major research done on centenarians. Researchers at the University of Georgia concluded that the common denominators among these one-hundred-year-olds were ability to suffer loss of younger family members and spouses; connection to community; humor; and faith in God! The number one commonality was the ability to move on after suffering significant loss. We certainly can't prevent the loss of family members as we get older, but we can perhaps do some preparatory inventory work about what loss represents to us. Studies reveal that women generally outlive their husbands. But when the wife precedes the husband, the man does not usually live much longer without his wife. This should cause us as men to look seriously at the issues in our marriages and what the nurture of the wife represents. Perhaps we can do some preventive work by becoming our own nurturers or broadening our base of relationships so that the loss does not take the devastating toll on us that it normally would.

Reconciliation

It would seem that the key to experiencing *zaken* as the most fulfilling time of life is in having our important relationships maintained and reconciled. During the early stages of adult manhood, we can alienate a lot of people. Warriors are not known for their sensitivity to family members, employees, or distant relatives. Men who are still phallic as adults can ruin their marriages through sexual indiscretions and affairs. These in turn can turn children against their father for hurting and disgracing their mother. The wounded male can so pull into this life that loved ones finally give up trying to reach him and move on—usually with much anger or regret for what they wish they could have had from him. In other words, we men can make a mess of our primary relationships during our young and middle-adult years. To make our last years of life satisfying, we should do our best to reconcile any relationships severed or harmed in our earlier years. Good relationships should be nurtured and maintained by whatever means possible.

I am often amazed at how God sometimes uses secular sources to communicate His truth better than Christian ones. Two popular songs being aired daily on the secular pop stations as I write are both about reconciliation. One is a song by Phil Collins entitled, "You're No Son of Mine." Whether it is autobiographical or not, I'm not sure. But it is about a man in later life who remembers how his own father rejected him, saying, "You're no son of mine." In response, he leaves and doesn't come back. But in midlife, he makes the attempt to reconcile. I say *attempt*, because that's all it is, an attempt. When he returns after many years to his father, the father repeats the refrain, "You're no son of mine." When I hear the song, it yanks my heart out about both the stubbornness of the father and the pain and wound the son still feels as an adult.

The other song is the one quoted in an earlier chapter by Elton John, entitled, "The Last Song." It is about a father who comes to his son while he is dying of AIDS. The son is as fragile as a bird, feeling pain under his skin, anger seething out of every pore for not being able to win but seeing his destiny to lose. His father opens the windows to let fresh air in, holds his son to his chest, and they speak of the things they had never spoken of before. The son's conclusion: "I guess I misjudged a father's love for his son." Tears come to my eyes even as I write these words. Why is this? Is it because I am a father with a son, or because I know several with this horrible disease, or is it even deeper? The first two are of course part of it, but it is still deeper. What we have in both of these songs is the universal theme of reconciliation. It's a divine theme. All men, being made in the image of God, have the innate desire to see fractured relationships mended and healed. This is the stuff that the best novels, dramas, movies, and songs are made of. It's the universal story of redemption and reconciliation that begins with God and has been placed in our consciences through creation. When that innate desire is resisted and rejected, we reap tragic, long-term consequences. When accepted, healing flows at the deepest of levels.

I know a man in his late fifties who is making this attempt. He has grown children. While in his thirties, he developed drinking problems; his wife left and took the kids. It was anything but an amicable divorce. She prevented the children from having any real contact with their father, and so for twenty years there was little communication. In his early fifties, John discovered a personal faith with Christ and found out about reconciliation. Being reconciled with God was just the first step of many in trying to reconcile his past relationships. He told me recently that his adult kids are still having difficulty accepting their "changed" father, but at least there is renewed contact after twenty years. He is being a grandfather to his sons' children and they are overjoyed to have his presence in their lives. The healing will be slow but I applaud his efforts. He is being a *zaken* in focusing on his primary relationships and trying to reconcile and maintain them.

Being a *zaken* also means making the most significant contribution of one's life.

Zaken as Time of Significant Contribution

We men are often shortsighted and in a hurry. However, studies of great men seldom reflect the popular vision of the twenty-nine-year-old millionaire. If we think life is over at forty, fifty, sixty, seventy, or even at eighty, we're wrong! Levinson notes,

> Some of the greatest intellectual and artistic works have been produced by men in their sixties, seventies, and even eighties. Examples abound: Picasso, Yeats, Verdi, Frank Lloyd Wright, Sigmund Freud, Carl Jung, Sophocles, Michelangelo, Tolstoy. Countless other men have contributed their wisdom as elders in a variety of counseling, educative and supporting roles in family and community.[6]

To Levinson's I can add my own list of late-life heroes, older men who have mentored me from a distance by their writings. Men such as C. S. Lewis, writing after the death of his wife; Alexander Solzhenitsyn, writing after his captivity in the Gulag; Elton Trueblood; Oswald Sanders; and a French scholar in his seventies, Jacques Ellul. I'm so glad these men didn't think life was over at forty, fifty, sixty, or seventy.

The *zaken* of Israel were not only men who by their age had obtained life's wisdom, but they were the ones looked to for advice, administrative insight, and judgment. As a smart king, David courted the *zaken* of Judah (1 Samuel 10:1-5). Often the *zaken* of regions and cities were called together to defend their region (Judges 11:5-11), families, and cities

(2 Kings 10:1-5). Many passages underscore the role of *zaken* in furnishing counsel along with the priests and prophets (Job 12:20, Jeremiah 18:18, Ezekiel 7:26). In the book of Deuteronomy, the *zaken* in particular made critical administrative decisions and effected reconciliation for people at odds with each other. These decisions governed issues such as capital punishment (21:1-9), marriages (25:5-10), and settling marital disputes (Ezra 10:8,14). The *zaken* apparently had some official capacity to oversee the faithful administration of the law (Deuteronomy 31:9,28).

In summary, the biblical data reflect the *zaken* involved in every aspect of society. They symbolize the unity and solidarity of the nation as one people of God (Numbers 11). They are found sitting at the gates of the cities discussing the political, civic, and religious affairs of the day (Deuteronomy 19:12, 21:2; Ruth 4:2,4,9,11; and Proverbs 31:23). Knowing human nature, I believe the younger men and boys were doubtlessly perched not far away, listening in and watching from a distance, when these older men of the culture gathered at the gates. Just as a young man today might look at a company president's lush office and say to himself, "That's where I will sit someday," so we see these young men looking at this group of *zaken* as the mentor models of manhood and saying, "Someday I'll sit at the city gates!"

If this time of life is characterized by significant contribution, probably the greatest contribution lies in the mentoring experience. In the last years of life, what hopefully began in the *'ish* stage has its greatest fulfillment here. Having one's own family raised and having the experience of life, the man has the most to give to the younger. Today there seems to be a growing realization among younger men that they need the active intervention of older men in their lives.

Mentoring
In almost every field today the concept of mentoring is being discussed. It is as if a major corrective move is now taking place in business, industry, and educational circles. In the

past it seemed everyone was content to pursue career goals individually without considering the role of others who might enhance the process. On the other hand, in many companies the problem was at the top. Bosses either "stole" the ideas and vision of the younger men or viewed them as threats to their own job security. Consequently, for a boss to form a relationship that would not only focus on the younger warrior's job requirements but also get into life goals that could lead to even more successes was unthinkable. Now many of these mentoring relationships are actually formed *within* the contexts of companies.[7]

At Seminary of the East, where I teach, we have applied this mentoring approach to theological education. Every student has at least two older mentors with whom he can meet weekly to share lives, discuss ministry, and look at what is being learned in the academic setting. In order to better facilitate these mentoring relationships, we solicited the help of The Uncommon Individual Foundation. They research existing mentoring programs and act as consultants to those desirous of implementing such. From this interaction our faculty has learned much about the dynamics of mentoring. These dynamics hold true in any kind of relationship where an older man seeks to invest his life in younger men. The foundation defines this process as "the phenomenon where people just starting out need three things to succeed: a dream (goal, ambition, vision, plan); someone who believes in them and can help bring their dream to reality; and determination. Mentors are then helpers who are there, but not necessarily the ensurers of success."[8]

We have found that the mentor contributes several things to his students: a brain to pick, a shoulder to cry on, and an occasional kick in the pants. Beyond this, the mentor cares for the younger man in the *totality* of his life and wants to see him become successful in life. I believe this is the greatest need in the church today. So many younger men in our churches need to hear the voices of older men in some context besides church business meetings. They need the one-on-one, the life experience, the realism of what life was like for them at the same age. Without this mentoring, men either "go it alone" or go it with others who don't know what they are doing!

Levinson places a realistic value on *zaken* kind of mentoring: "Being a mentor with young adults is one the most significant relationships available to a man in middle adulthood," if on the other side of the relationship "the protégé can come to appreciate and tolerate the mentor's human frailties, and if the two of them can find a mutual basis for being friends, or colleagues."[9]

So what biblical character do we think of who made this kind of investment in someone younger? Two come to mind immediately: Elijah with Elisha, and Abraham.

Elijah and Elisha as the *Zaken* Relationship

In the last chapter, I characterized Elijah as an *'ish* kind of man who, having recovered from his wounding after the Jezebel incident, left the cave in the Sinai. God told him to anoint a new prophet, Elisha. Therefore, the remainder of Elijah's life is a study of the relationship between these two men. It is a study of mentoring. Elijah, knowing that his ministry would not continue in the same way or last very long, focuses his attention on his replacement (1 Kings 19:16,21). In this relationship we see a renewed boldness in Elijah as he confronts Ahab and his incumbent, Joram. But the main thrust of his efforts during this time is on the Elijah-Elisha relationship.

This mentoring is pursued by Elisha, who will not leave Elijah's side (2 Kings 2:2,4,6). One of the things we have learned in our program is that for mentoring to be successful, it must be protégé-driven. If the student doesn't really embrace it and learn how to recognize a good mentor, our best efforts are in vain! Elisha is aggressive and won't let Elijah off the hook. At one point, Elijah finally asks Elisha what it is he wants (2:9). In his typical aggressive spirit Elisha answers, "A double portion of your spirit." Quite a request, but Elijah complies, saying, in effect, if you hang around long enough to see me go, you will have it (2:10). As they are still walking together, a chariot of fire shows up and carries Elijah off. As the chariot rises, Elijah leans out and throws Elisha his rolled-up mantle that he had used to part the waters of the Jordan. Elisha picks it up, goes back to the Jordan, and strikes the waters with the mantle, and they part. The mantle has been passed, the work will go on—all because of the mentoring relationship. It was Elijah's final earthly contribution, and what a great one. So it can be for every *zaken* (usually without the special effects, though).

Abraham as *Zaken*

Abraham is a little different story. Here we see a *zaken* in his elder responsibility to his family. In this sense he is the model of maintaining the family connection so important at this station of life. He certainly made his share of family mistakes, though. He couldn't wait for the promise of God, so he took Hagar, Sarah's handmaiden, and raised up an offspring from her, which only caused many long-term problems (Genesis 16). He had to separate from his nephew Lot, which only got Lot into some other long-term problems (Genesis 14, 19). When in Gerar, he lied to the king about his own wife by calling her his sister. As I understand this passage, more was going on here than meets the eye. We are told Abimelech, thinking Sarah was Abraham's sister, "takes her" (Genesis 20:2). Since much time passes, I believe she became a part of Abimelech's sexual harem, though the text says they never had relations. At any rate, this may have been Abraham's attempt to dump Sarah for not giving him any children! We know some time had lapsed because it says that no one in Abimelech's household could be pregnant (20:17). At any rate, Abraham is eventually found out and he gets Sarah back. I wonder what she said after that?

Then God finally carries out His promise and Sarah conceives Isaac. Abraham is now 100 years old. But when Isaac is grown, God tells Abraham to offer up his promised son (22:2). Now I must confess, I'm not sure I could do this. No, I know I couldn't do it. It's even unthinkable for me that God would ask such a thing. It seems nothing but unjust, uncaring, violent, and sinister. It makes God seem to be an arbitrary, whimsical, malevolent deity. But He asks it of Abraham. And Abraham, with his adult son, goes along with it and passes the test (22:12). To me this is the greatest expression of faith in the Bible. Then Sarah dies, leaving Abraham alone with Isaac at age 130-something (23:1).

As a really old *zaken*, Abraham's concern is for the continuance of his family. The remainder of the story of Abraham's life is devoted to a lengthy development of getting Isaac a proper bride (24:1-5). I see this as reflecting the *zaken* concern for making sure the family connections are right before Abraham can die in peace. He can die full of years and in peace because his progeny is in place. By the way, after Sarah's death we are told that he remarries and even has more children (25:1-4), but leaves everything to Isaac. What happened to his impotency problem? Apparently, in biblical times there was sex for men in their 100s! Now that's a fulfilled man.

I have seen precious few true-to-life *zakens* in my own life. It may be my own limited experience, but two come to mind immediately. Each of these men used his retirement to be thoroughly connected with his community and church, where each made a significant contribution during these years, even though he remained unknown to most.

The first was "Grandpastor," as he was affectionately called by everyone. He was the dean of the college where I taught right out of seminary. He had helped his son, the pastor of a church and later president of the college, start the college out of nothing. Dr. J. W. Cook's evening Bible classes soon became the beginning of a four-year Bible college. All this while in his seventies and twice retired — first from the mission field, and then from Western Seminary where he had taught missions. His silver-white hair made him the elder statesman of both the congregation and the college. I still remember the day he reported to us that the doctor had found cancer in his aging body. I asked him, "What are you going to do?" He replied, "Just keep on living." And he did, even with cancer, at least another ten years, which put him into his eighties. Grandpastor died a true *zaken*, full of years and full of protégés, one of them being me.

My other *zaken* is still contributing. Paul took early retirement, but since then he has been far from confined to golf courses or retirement homes. He could have been content to sit in church, listen to sermons, and start to slide for home. But that's not Paul. When most evangelical churches wanted nothing to do with divorced persons, Paul and his wife Phyllis began to reach out to them. They opened their home to the divorced, single adults, and single parents. They fed them, listened to their difficulties, and over the years have probably hosted hundreds of divorced adults in their home. Paul and Phyllis worked behind the scenes with men and women, while also doing the financial accounting for what has now become an international divorce-recovery seminar, Fresh Start. They are connected and have contributed to more people than most full-time pastors I know. Even though physical difficulties and chemotherapy have become a regular part of Paul's life, he has slowed only a little. A couple of years ago, a few of us got together to have a surprise "thank you" for these real-life mentors. It was my honor to award them as a joke an "honorary divorce" from each other, since they had helped so many through this period of time. It is the only divorce I hope I ever have to preside over. Paul and Phyllis Malone, thanks for not believing life is over at fifty, or sixty! Your contribution continues, and I praise you for it.

As a professor at Dallas Seminary, Dr. Howard Hendricks always passed out an anonymous paper—"Advice to a (Bored) Young Man"—to every one of his students. I pass it on to you.

Died, age 20; buried, age 60. The sad epitaph of too many Americans. Mummification sets in on too many young men at an age when they should be ripping the world wide open. For example: Many people reading this page are doing so with the aid of bifocals. Inventor? B. Franklin, age 70. The presses that printed this page were powered by electricity. One of the harnessors? B. Franklin, age 40. Some are reading this on the campus of one of the Ivy League universities. Founder? B. Frank-

lin, age 46. Others, in a library. Who founded the first
library in America? B. Franklin, age 25. Some got their
copy through the U.S. Mail. Its father? B. Franklin, age
31. Now think fire. Who started the first fire department, invented the lightning rod, designed a heating
stove still in use today? B. Franklin, age 31, 43, 36. Wit,
Conversationalist, Economist, Philosopher, Diplomat,
Favorite of the capitals of Europe. Journalist, Printer,
Publisher, Linguist (spoke and wrote five languages).
Advocate of paratroopers (from balloon) a century
before the airplane was invented. All this until age 84.
And he had exactly two years of formal schooling. It's
a good bet that you already have more knowledge than
Franklin ever had when he was your age. Perhaps you
think there's no use trying to think of anything new,
that everything's been done. Wrong. The simple, agrar-
ian America of Franklin's day didn't begin to need the
answers we need today. *Do something about it!* Tear out
his page and read it on your 84th birthday. Ask yourself
what took over in your life, indolence or ingenuity!

The *zaken* keeps connecting, keeps contributing, and
makes reconciliations. So how do we put all this together?
What are some of the things we need at every point on the
masculine journey? Who can be a model for us at every stop?
That's where both the journey and the book end.

CHAPTER EIGHT

A New Male Journey

◆

And ah for a man to arise in me
That the man I am may cease to be!

LORD ALFRED TENNYSON
Maud

DICK TYRE, THE consultant I worked with at The Uncommon Individual Foundation, has divided people and organizations into two types — Dorothy types and Winnie-the-Pooh types. Taken from *The Wizard of Oz*, Dorothys are those who like to stay on the yellow-brick road, keep moving, and can't wait to get where they are going. Winnie-the-Poohs just enjoy the trip, the people they meet along the way, and the experiences. They feel a little regret when the trip is over. At my current stage of life, I am more of a Winnie-the-Pooh than a Dorothy.

I feel the same way about this book. The Dorothy part of me kept me writing and meeting deadlines. But I am really a Winnie-the-Pooh, who likes to enjoy the trip, so coming to the end is always the hardest part for me. But now I want to conclude by trying to look at these six stages on the male journey from a bird's-eye view. Each stop along the way is uniquely different for each man, but they all have some important commonalities. Just as each stage has some crucial new issues a man must face, so also each stage demands some new applications of faith. Finally, to whom do we look as the ultimate masculine model at each of these stages?

Common Characteristics of Each Stage

As mentioned in chapter 1, each of these stages will entail a certain amount of confusion. When I get lost on many of my travels, I find myself confused about which direction to go, who to ask directions from, and whether to trust the directions I get. So it is on this masculine journey.

Confusion

The *'adam* kind of man may be confused by having to unravel and integrate the paradoxes of human potentiality and our sinful tendencies. Others may struggle more with the confusion that confronting their own mortality can bring. Still others may have difficulty accepting the fact that many of their unfulfilled yearnings will never be satisfied.

For the phallic male, the *zakar*, confusion may exist in the emerging adolescent's sexuality. Understanding wet dreams, masturbation, and intercourse can be simultaneously very scary and exciting for young men. For the adult male, phallic confusion may exist in struggling to understand what is normal. Whether married or not, the issue of what is normative for the Christian male is often not clear. For an older adult, the confusion may lie in whether his sexuality will wane or in a fear that he will never again have the phallic kind of experiences he desires, and consequently what to do with that.

The *gibbor*, the warrior, may suffer confusion in trying to bring strength and intimacy together. How can he be the warrior but still care about people? Can the marketplace warrior really succeed in business while maintaining intimacy with his family? Does one have to sacrifice one's family to be successful today?

The *enosh*, the wounded male, wonders if he is really a man. How can he be weak and experience the kind of pain he feels and also be masculine? For him, this is a confusing time. He wonders if he will ever feel any different and how he can move out from where he is.

The mature man experiences confusion about what to do with the rest of his life. *'Ish* knows he needs to make some critical decisions, but he doesn't want to make the wrong ones. It is also threatening and confusing to think about how to start the reconnecting process with the people he loves. At the same time he may feel confused knowing he no longer has the same energy or tolerance for many of the things he could do earlier.

For the *zaken*, the elder man, confusion may set in as he prepares to die. Will he die well? Will he die alone? How will his family do without him? These are the questions that focus the *zaken's* confusion. He may struggle with faithfulness to God or be confused as to how his financial resources may care for him.

Confusion is normative for the masculine journey as you move from one stage to another. Don't let the confusion be a problem for you. This is transition time, and transitions always breed confusion.

Transition

Transition time means that there are no pure stages on this journey. No man is purely phallic, warrior, or sage. We are always making transitions between many of these stages every day. Fundamentally, we live in many towns at once, but one stage will predominate for a time. The lust of *zakar*, the fire of *gibbor*, the wound of *enosh*, the maturity of *ish*, and hopefully the wisdom of *zaken*—each is a part of me every day. But each of us spends a significant amount of time making transitions from one preeminent stage to another. Transitions are also common, normative. I do not believe we ever completely grow out of earlier stages, even though there is a conscious separation from previous stops.

Separation

I hope that you have benefited from this approach to understanding masculine psychology and theology. In the men's retreats I have done, men have told me they appreciated most seeing where their life at the moment fit on the overall map. This exercise forces men to deal with separation issues. When a man recognizes he is still a phallic kind of guy, it forces him to deal with the phallic issues in his life; only then can he move on and grow up a little. This means saying goodbye to the phallic stop as the city where he has lived and breathed and had his being. So it is with every stage.

Movement on this journey doesn't just happen. It takes some conscious effort to see where you are and separate from the characteristics, emotions, and behaviors of that stage. Without separation it is easy to make any one stop a permanent home, put down roots, and live there forever. In my mind this is a tragedy because there is so much more to the masculine journey that a stationary man, spinning his wheels, would miss. So keep separating and keep moving. One thing that helps us to separate is finding some self-imposed initiation rite to celebrate getting to the next stage.

Initiation

As discussed in so many men's books today, we men have lost all of our formal initiation rites. In their absence, the peer group usually substitutes negative ones: things like smoking one's first cigarette, getting drunk, or bedding a girl. These are now the most common adolescent male initiation rites. Adult ones are even more obscure or perverted: "Real men make money, play around, kill animals, cheat on their taxes, etc." Yet historically, initiation has always been a ceremonial aspect of manhood. Women don't have to prove anything to be a "real woman." The terms don't even go together and are never mentioned by either women or men. Men have to prove something. So, let's at least begin thinking about which appropriate initiation rites might fit each of these stages.

In a sense, our birthday is our first initiation rite to the '*adam* stage. But there might be some way we could make more ceremonial the first rich awareness of our mortality and utter sinfulness. I greatly appreciate how my parents made a "big deal" out of my first going under the knife when I was nine. Having my appendix taken out was my first graphic experience of feeling my own mortality. They recorded it with pictures and celebration. I still have the photos of that young, skinny, scared kid. But now it seems like it was more of an initiation rite for me. Maybe I accept pain better now because of it.

I'm sure many would balk at my thought of celebrating the experience of sin. I'm not sure how we could do it. But I do know we need to do it. For example, we usually give the teenagers in our churches such a massive dose of condemnation regarding their first experiences with sin that I sometimes wonder how any of them ever recover. Maybe we could take a different approach. Instead of jumping all over them when they have their first experience with the police, or their first drunk, or their first experience with sex or drugs, we could look upon this as a teachable moment and a rite of passage. Is this putting a benediction on sin? Of course not, but perhaps at this point the true elders could come forward and confess their own adolescent sins and congratulate the next generation for being human. Then they could move on to the all-important issues of forgiveness and restoration, but this time on common ground, with the young person as a fellow sinner!

In some cultures there is far more phallic initiation than in ours. Ours usually happen in the back seats of automobiles or, in today's latchkey society, in the parents' homes! Certainly, God has programed some of the initiation by designing our male bodies to grow pubic hair and have wet dreams. Should we celebrate such things with our sons? It would certainly be embarrassing for most boys I know! But do you realize that in some cultures, on the wedding night, while everyone is dancing and celebrating at the reception, the groom takes his new bride to a chamber off to the side, has intercourse with her to consummate the marriage, and then returns to the party?

When the happy couple returns, everyone applauds and offers a round of more drinks! The couple has been initiated into the phallic arena. At least it is something to think about.

Traditionally, the initiation rite for the warrior has been the first kill — whether fighter pilot, deerhunter, or headhunter. Perhaps we do celebrate this one more than the others. Our athletic competitions award medals, ribbons, and trophies to celebrate similar victories. Companies give their trips, perks, and bonuses to new employees who bag their first sales trophy. Yet I wonder how we might find some appropriate ways of rewarding and making some spiritual-warrior benchmarks for our men. When a man has achieved some major spiritual victory in his life, how can we celebrate it or honor him as a warrior for Christ? I have no answers here, only questions. But I believe we do need to affirm this developmental stage along the masculine journey.

If ever we needed to initiate the wounded in our midst it is now. We need to recognize a man's divorce, or job firing, or major health problem, or culpability in some legal or sexual indiscretion, as a wound to which we show deference as a part of the male journey. Again, am I saying we place a benediction on sin? Again, I say no! We are just giving men a better frame in which to see the event. Instead of burying the wound, or denying its pain, or having friends and the church turn away from the injured man, we need to see these experiences as potentially significant maturing events. They can be initiation rites to lead men to a higher and richer level of masculine spiritual life.

For the mature man, we must learn to celebrate his great expressions of faith in launching out on a new career, or seeking important family reconciliation. A man's attempt to spend more time with his family or rebuild relationships is something to be honored with an initiation rite of some sort. We might even consider celebrating the release of old illusions that formerly only got a man into trouble. These signs of maturity deserve the appropriate initiation rites to becoming an *ish*.

For the sage, many of the initiation components are

already built into the physical body. Graying hair, going bald, wearing glasses, and retirement are humorously talked about. Retirement parties are common. But the intent is usually focused on all the wrong things. It is viewed as ending something significant and moving into something less demanding and slower paced. In the church we could celebrate any man (or couple) who is willing to take a risk at this late stage of life, start a new business, run for office, take on a new ministry, or open their home for the youth of the church. These should be initiation rites because they express what being a *zaken* is all about.

The above characterizes the common elements of each stage on this journey. In addition, there are a few things that each stage needs in order to facilitate the transition from one place to another.

What Is Needed at Each Stage

When I teach on the male journey at conferences and retreats, the question I receive more than any other at the conclusion is, "How does one keep moving on the journey, and keep from being stuck?" I use the illustration of Elijah to answer. When he ran from Jezebel and hid out in the desert cave, what moved him on? What got him back into the mainstream? It took a special messenger of the Lord (an angel) to minister to him, and the very voice of God in a small, still voice to move him. Finally, it took Elijah believing the message, trusting in it, and getting up and moving out of the cave. So I believe it is at each stop on the journey. We need a mentor, a voice from God, and a unique expression of faith.

A Mentor Keeps Us Moving

Wherever I am on the masculine journey, I need a mentor who is at least one stage ahead of me, I need this to provide a model of masculinity at the next stage and the encouragement I need to leave where I am and grow up a little. If I am a phallic college guy enjoying the sexual pleasures women bring me, I need an older man who may be a warrior in adult life, to show me how to channel or translate my sexual energy into something more constructive like business or a career. When I am a warrior drawing blood from everyone around me, I need a wounded man to come alongside and give me the perspective I need to see that one day *I* may be the one who is bleeding. When I think I *am bleeding to death*, I need a mature man to take some pity on me, bandage my wounds, and give me the hope I need to survive. Knowing he has survived similar wounding and moved on with his life may be all I need to move on. When I'm an *ish* kind of man, I know what life is about, and it becomes so easy to isolate and just do what I want to do with my life. At that point I need a sage to give me a vision for my life that includes reconnecting with people, reconciling with people I may have written off, loving my enemies, and making a contribution from my life experience. I hope when I am a *zaken*, someone will be around to help me die well. Maybe that's when God alone is my mentor!

I must say the past few years have been the most difficult for me. I believe it is simply because I have not had the mentor during this stage in my life. Fortunately, this is the first stage I've been without one. I have had the phallic, warrior, and wounded mentors. But the mature mentor whom I have needed has not been there. In most of my primary relations I have been the oldest, being a mentor to others. It seems I haven't found those who were mature, honest, and confident enough that I could genuinely trust them with my inner life. This is new for me on my journey and I feel the vacuum significantly. But this is what we need God for.

Seeing Jesus as the Voice of God

The second most often-asked question I get at men's retreats is, "Where does Jesus fit into all this?" Well, He fits very nicely as the One who moves us on from one stage to the next. He is the only One who can genuinely empathize with where we are because He also has experienced the same stages on the masculine journey (Hebrews 4:15). Jesus, of course, was the second Adam (Romans 5:14), and as the second Adam was very much human, He experienced the full range of human emotional and physical life, yet did not sin. But the Hebrews passage affirms for us that He was sincerely tempted to sin. I believe He was truly tempted without compromising His deity.

Jesus was also very much *zakar*, phallic. As much as the feminists try to ignore this issue, Jesus was very much masculine, and masculine means being male, and being male means having a penis. There's no way around it. Some in church history could not tolerate the exposure of the Son of God's genitalia. Therefore, you will never find a portrait of the crucifixion of Jesus with penis exposed, even though it was a common Roman custom to crucify criminals naked. Even the gospel writers tell us that Jesus' outward garment was torn into four pieces, leaving the inner tunic, which was then gambled for intact (John 19:23-24). That left nothing. No underpants. Nothing. And I seriously doubt that the soldiers would have wrapped a towel around Him for the sake of the portrait!

I believe Jesus was phallic with all the inherent phallic passions we experience as men. But it was never recorded that Jesus had sexual relations with a woman. He may have thought about it as the movie *The Last Temptation of Christ* portrays, but even in this movie He did not give in to the temptation and remained true to His messianic course. If temptation means anything, it means Christ was tempted in *every* way as we are. That would mean not only heterosexual temptation but also homosexual temptation! I have found this insight to be very helpful for gay men struggling with their sexuality.

We certainly see Christ as the warrior from day one of His messianic career. He wars against the Pharisees; He wars for the sake of the sinner, the outcast, women, children, and His Father's house. This last act of the warrior probably got Him crucified (Matthew 21:12,45). He warred for the truth, for the true meaning of the Law and its application, for compassion, for justice, and for the sake of His Father's will. If we need a spiritual warrior as a model, then we see it perfectly in the life of Christ.

For men who are experiencing woundedness, Jesus again

is our model. We see Him as a wounded male, struggling with His Father's will in the Garden of Gethsemane (Luke 22:39-45). He struggled with the disciples into whom He had poured His life, but who then betrayed Him (22:47-62). Next, His own humiliation before the leaders and populace of the nation was a public wound (22:63–23:25). With the crucifixion, His wounding was complete — it was a wound unto death. He was broken, bruised, bleeding, and dying. No matter how beaten down we men may feel, Jesus has been there before us. He knows and understands what it is like and can be the voice of God to us about it.

In the resurrection, we can see Jesus as the mature man, reconnecting with His disciples, encouraging them in their disillusionment (24:13-49), and bringing about reconciliation with Peter who denied Him (John 21:1-25). The Risen Lord has become the ruler not only of His own soul, but also of the universe. The resurrection proves that Christ is the Ruler of life, capable of bringing about restoration in the worst of situations. This is the voice of God to men at this stage on the map: He can do the impossible, He can be the reconciler, and He can be trusted for new pursuits.

Jesus is also seen as our sage. Even though he only lived to the age of thirty-three, He was wise beyond His years. He knew when leaving His work on earth that He must involve Himself in mentoring the men who would carry on His work after He departed. So from day one His focus was on the Twelve in teaching, training, and preparing them for the time He would leave (Mark 3:13-19, 6:7-13, 10:33). He functioned as their sage, their elder, their mentor, giving them a vision for the work they would undertake in finishing the work He started (John 14:18, 21:17). He even prepared them for His continuing work in their lives by giving them the promise of His own Spirit, who would return to indwell their consciousness (16:7-15). Likewise, for the voice I need at this stage of life I can look to Jesus as the model. He is my sage, my mentor, and continuous contributor to my life and others.

Jesus is the voice we need at every stage on the male

journey to help pull us out of our caves and get us moving forward on our journeys. He has always been before us, no matter where we are. He can be trusted as our guide. But I still have to place my faith in Him at every point on the journey.

New Expressions of Faith at Every Stage

Current developmental literature records a debate as to whether faith is something to be developed throughout the adult life cycle in the same way that Levinson, Erickson, Maslow, Piaget, and Kohlberg have conceived development in the other areas of adult life (physical, psychological, intellectual, and moral).[1] I am not an expert on such subjects, but I do have an opinion. It seems to me that, rather than being something that goes through different developmental stages as in cognitive or moral development, *faith is something that is uniquely required at each point on our developmental journey.* I believe each stop on the journey is different and consequently calls for a unique expression of faith in order to effect progress. But faith is faith. We either trust Christ for what we are facing or we don't. At every point on the journey I can be faithful or unfaithful. I can be just as unfaithful as a sage as in the phallic stage. Faith is always moment by moment, day by day, event by event, and stage by stage. I wish I could reach a certain level of faith and then stay there, but this has not been my experience, nor do I believe this is biblical. At every point on the journey I face some unique area that demands a new expression of faith.

As a phallic man, I need to trust God with my sexuality, whether young or old. For a younger man, this means waiting on God for the right woman with whom you want to spend the rest of your life. For the married man, it means by faith continuing to trust God with your sexuality and reserving it for the wife of your youth. Whatever our sexual struggles are, we are all prone to infidelity and immortality, so the requirement of faith is the same. We must trust God with our phallus, and seek to be pleasing to Him in accordance with His revealed guidance.

For the warrior, I must trust God with the wars I fight. There are many wars that need to be fought and some that are not worth losing any blood over. When I go to war—whether for truth, justice, or compassion—I need to trust God for the strength needed to wage the war faithfully and whole-heartedly. A man needs a sword and the sword must be sharp. But I also need to trust Christ with the area of not shedding innocent blood. I need His guidance to wage war ethically and morally.

When I am wounded I need to trust Christ with my wounds. I need to believe that healing is possible and there is a way out. I can survive. During this time it is easy to feel hopeless and unable to see Christ at all. This is the toughest faith. At some points it seems like mere faith in faith. That's when I trust God even though I can see no evidence of His presence or activity. In this expression of faith, over time, we begin to hear the quiet voice of Christ calling us out.

The mature man needs to express his faith in Christ as the renewer and reconciler of his vision. As he launches out on new pursuits, he needs to trust his mentor who has called him out. This is Abraham lifting up his most prized possession, and going out from a city he knew very well to one he wasn't quite sure of. The mature man needs daily expressions of faith as well, to keep moving on the journey.

It would be nice to believe that by the time you become a sage, you would not need any more unique expressions of faith. But perhaps with declining health, seeing loved ones pass away, and leaving one's life work to others, our natural tendency is to become very fearful. Therefore, a new expression of faith is needed here to live out the last years, as well as to speed one home to his Maker. Then our Lord will say, "Well done, My faithful servant, you finished the race and ended well. Come on home and claim your reward as a man!"

All journeys are expressions of faith. The scenery changes, people come and go, cars pass us by, but we keep moving.

Sometimes we get lost or confused. Along the way we encounter some real joys and pleasures; other times, pain and discomfort. All are part of the journey. At some point in every man's life he must face the reality that the journey is more than a trip, it is a pilgrimage, a pilgrimage that ends with our Maker. For we travel to a city whose founder and maker is God.

> For a long time yet, led by some wondrous power, I am
> fated to journey hand in hand with my strange heroes
> and to survey the surging immensity of life, to survey
> it through the laughter that all can see and through the
> tears unseen and unknown by anyone.[2]

Doxa Christo!

Appendix

The Six Stages of Manhood			
	'Adam	Zakar	Gibbor
Chapter Title	Creational	Phallic	Warrior
Summary Idea	Noble savage	Mysterious taskmaster	Royal guardian
Orientation	Potentiality and mortality	Sexual activity, energy, and identity	Competing Winning Conquering
Initiation Rituals	Birth Sickness Injury Aging	Wet dreams Pubic hair Masturbation Intercourse	First blood First win, sale First conflict
Unique Needs	Seeing capabilities Accepting limitations	Regulation and cultivation of desires Sublimation	Courage Strength Moral conscience
Role of Mentor	Believes in abilities Reminds about limitations	Affirms biblical sexuality	Calls forth strength Offers ethical insight
Image Symbol	Eden's tree	Enlarged penis	Sword
Biblical Character	Solomon	Samson	David
Contemporary Illustrations	Inside traders Shylock televangelists	Hugh Hefner Ernest Hemingway	Oliver North Donald Trump Martin Luther King
Application of Faith	Trusting God with mortality and capabilities	Trusting God with sexual desires and regulations	Trusting God for courage and moral conscience
Example of Jesus	New or second Adam Romans 5:14	Temptation as a male Hebrews 4:15	Warrior for His Father's concerns Matthew 21:12

The Six Stages of Manhood (*cont.*)		
Enosh	**Ish**	**Zaken**
Wounded	Mature	Sage
Wounded warrior	Knows and rules himself	Mentor
Pain, hurt Grief Depression	Reconnecting Reframing Refocusing	Reconciliation Contribution Mentoring
Significant loss Defeat, failure Divorce Disease	New career Marriage Re-establishing relationship	Running for office Reconciliating family Coaching little league
Permission to grieve, articulate pain	Healing Direction Vision	Endurance Encouragement by peers and younger people
Grants permission Offers insight on pain	Affirms wounds Recasts vision	Just being there
Open wound Blood	Small, still voice Horeb's cave	Mantle passed Gray hair City gates
Job Jacob	Elijah	Elijah, Elisha Abraham
Jim Bakker Vietnam vets Iran Contra indictees	Elie Weizel Alexandre Solzhenitsyn Chuck Colson	C. S. Lewis Robert Bly Malcolm Muggeridge
Seeing God in the wound, accepting a purpose for the pain	Trusting God with uncertainty and new direction	Trusting God with declining health, loss, and investment in the young
Gethsemene Humiliation Crucifixion Rejection Luke 22–23	Resurrection Reconnecting and encouraging disciples Luke 24	Mentoring, empowering, and envisioning His disciples Matthew 28:16-20

Notes

◆

Dedication
1. A paraphrase of King Solomon in Psalm 127.

Chapter One: An Uneasy Men's Movement
1. "A man must go on a quest to discover the sacred fire in the sanctuary of his own belly, to ignite the flame in his heart, to fuel the blaze in the hearth, to rekindle his ardor for the earth," Sam Keen, *Fire in the Belly* (New York: Bantam Books, 1991), page 1.
2. Robert Bly, *Iron John* (Reading, MA: Addison-Wesley, 1990).
3. Robert A. Johnson, *He: Understanding Male Psychology* (New York: Harper and Row, 1974), page 3.
4. Samuel Osherson, *Finding Our Fathers* (New York: The Free Press, 1986).
5. Deborah Tannen, *You Just Don't Understand* (New York: Ballantine Books, 1990).
6. Men's primary fantasy is having access to as many beautiful women as possible without risk of rejection. Women's primary fastasy is financial security and family, which is obtained by her beauty and sexual power. Warren Farrell, *Why Men Are the Way They Are* (New York: Berkley Books, 1986), page 18.
7. See a conversation with Robert Bly in Keith Thompson, ed., *To Be a Man: In Search of the Deep Masculine* (Los Angeles: Jeremy P. Tarcher, 1991), page 21, where he says that the golden ball (key to manhood) does not lie with Jesus. Yet he ends his book *Iron John* by commenting on the observation of French therapist Marie-Louise von

Franz, "She remarked that she has noticed in dreams of both men and women in recent decades a figure who is spiritual but also covered with hair, a sort of hairy Christ. She believes that what the psyche is asking for now is a new figure, a religious figure but a hairy one, in touch with God and sexuality, with spirit and earth," page 249.

8. Daniel J. Levinson, *The Seasons of a Man's Life* (New York: Ballantine Books, 1978).

9. Levinson, page 20.

10. See the following works for a thorough discussion of these differences: Tannen, *You Just Don't Understand*; Joe Tanenbaum, *Male and Female Realities* (Sugarland, TX: Candle Publishing, 1989); Herb Goldberg, *The Inner Male* (New York: Signet, 1987); Richard Restak, *The Brain: The Last Frontier* (New York: Warner Books, 1979); and Farrell, *Why Men Are the Way They Are*.

11. Thompson, page 3. What Thompson refers to is what modern linguists have identified as the "deep structures" in the human brain that make humans qualitatively different from animals in linguistic, or communication, ability. In recent years linguists like Noam Chomsky, Donald McKeon, Clifford Wilson, and others have shown that it is more than just vocal chord differences that enable humans to speak, but rather "deep structures" inherent in the human brain that are not there in other creatures. McKeon and Wilson record their findings in *The Language Gap* (Dallas, TX: Probe Books/Word Publishing, 1986). Thompson's point is that not only are the "deep structures" in humans generally different from the rest of earth's creatures, but that male "deep structures" are quite different from those of females within the human species. Another researcher in this area, Canadian anthropologist Arthur Custance, claims that these "deep structures" are evidence of the existence of the human soul. See Arthur Custance, *The Mysterious Matter of Mind* (Grand Rapids: MI: Zondervan/Probe, 1983).

Chapter 2: Creational Male — 'Adam

1. I will assume throughout the book what I consider a fact about the origin of humankind. The Scriptures assume as a first premise both the idea of God and the idea that He is the personal agent responsible for all the creation including mankind (Genesis 1:11, Psalm 89:47-48). Humanity is then the special creative handiwork of this Creator.

2. Akkadian background reveals *adamatu* and *adamu*, which mean "dark, red soil" and "red or blood," respectively, G. Johannes Botterwick and Helmer Ringgren, ed., *Theological Dictionary of the Old Testament*, vol. 1 (Grand Rapids: Eerdmans, 1974), pages 75-87.

3. Elton Trueblood, *Alternative to Futility* (Waco, TX: Word, 1948), page 40.

4. In the development, *'adam* is given the responsibility to name all the animals, but there was none found that seemed appropriate for a personal relationship. Only the woman, having been specially fashioned by God and brought to *'adam*, was found acceptable. Together they become the joyous ground for the institution of marriage. This profoundly argues against the modern gay movement and "alternative lifestyles" that try to "normalize" or legalize homosexual marriage and relationships. It also more subtly suggests that the dog is not man's best friend. An animal cannot provide for man what a woman can. *'Adam* rejoiced over Eve, not Steve or Spot!

5. Gail Sheehy, *The Silent Passage* (New York: Random House, 1992), page 43.

6. Anthony Storr, *Human Destructiveness* (New York: Ballantine Books, 1991), page 5.

7. Alexander Solzhenitsyn, *The Gulag Archipelago I* (New York: Harper and Row, 1973), page 168.

8. Even though the authorship of Ecclesiastes is debated, I believe all available evidence suggests Solomon as the writer.

9. When the accounts in 1 Kings and 2 Chronicles are

compared and amounts of gold and silver are noted, Solomon's own house was larger than the Temple and had far more material worth.

Chapter Three: The Phallic Male—*Zakar*

1. William L. Holladay, ed., *A Concise Hebrew and Aramaic Lexicon of the Old Testament* (Grand Rapids: Eerdmans, 1971), page 89.
2. See Brown, Driver, and Briggs, *A Hebrew and English Lexicon of the Old Testament*; and G. Johannes Botterwick and Helmer Ringgren, ed., *Theological Dictionary of the Old Testament*, vol. 4 (Grand Rapids: Eerdmans, 1974), pages 82-87.
3. Botterwick and Ringgren, page 83.
4. Botterwick and Ringgren, page 83.
5. Women were killed in the conquest of Canaan, but it seems this was not by the intent of what was declared in Deuteronomy.
6. Quoted in Eugene Monick, "Phallos and Religious Experience," in Keith Thompson, ed., *To Be a Man: In Search of the Deep Masculine* (Los Angeles: Jeremy P. Tarcher, 1991), page 127.
7. Nancy Qualls-Corbett, *The Sacred Prostitute: Eternal Aspect of the Feminine* (Toronto: Inner City Books, 1988), pages 39-40.
8. Monick, page 127.
9. Patrick Carnes, *Out of the Shadows* (Minneapolis: Comp-Care Publishers, 1983), pages 9, 16.
10. Sam Keen, *Fire in the Belly* (New York: Bantam Books, 1991), page 74.
11. See Holladay, page 87.
12. This is an interesting use of the word *orient*, today. To orient means literally to "make oriental" or to bend one toward the east, Oriental meaning east. Today, this joining of all differences into one semantic and sexual monism, or androgyny, is exactly what it means to turn east. That's what Eastern philosophy does, as

opposed to Judeo-Christianity, which always keeps the God/man distinction separate along with the male/female distinction.

13. The first time I read this passage I was appalled that anyone would ever consider having sex with an animal. However, reality eventually hits the most experienced of counselors. I had one man come to see me who revealed that he had contracted a very bad infection around his groin area. I asked him why he hadn't seen a doctor. He told me because he was afraid he had contracted a disease from sheep. The light bulb still didn't go on in my mind. I thought he was a farmer or something. Finally, he told me of his long-term practice of having sex with animals. I immediately got him in contact with a physician. When I did a sexual history with him, I found he, like many others with sexual problems, had been raped as his first sexual experience by an older cousin.

14. Joe Dallas, "Born Gay," *Christianity Today*, June 22, 1992, page 21.

15. "Can Homosexuals Change?" Family Research Institute survey of 4,340 adults, *The Family Report*, Washington, D.C.

16. Dr. Richard M. Restak states, "The most exciting and hopeful aspect of this whole thing, however, is that in some cases the ultimate sexual pattern can be significantly affected by the environment," *The Brain: The Last Frontier* (New York: Warner Books, 1979), page 228. He also notes, "Our conscious thoughts and actions are constantly modified by a barrage of signals from internal sources," Restak, *The Brain* (New York: Bantam, 1984), page 144. What this says to the present writer is, both our actions and thoughts about our sexual role have biochemical effects on our brain which in turn monitor our hormones. This is very close to the biblical notion of "as a man thinks, so he is" (Proverbs 23:7).

17. Leanne Payne, *The Healing of the Homosexual* (Westchester, IL: Crossway, 1985), page 37. Also see her larger

and more theoretical work, *The Broken Image* (Westchester, IL: Crossway, 1981), especially chapter 4, "The Search for Sexual Identity," pages 65-137.

18. W. Gunther Plaut, Bernard J. Bamberger, and William W. Hallo, *The Torah: A Modern Commentary* (New York: Union of American Hebrew Congregations, 1981), page 879.

19. John Barron, *Mig Pilot: The Final Escape of Lieutenant Belenko* (New York: McGraw-Hill, 1980).

20. See Matthew 5:28.

21. Warren Farrell, *Why Men Are the Way They Are* (New York: Berkley Books, 1986), page 18.

22. *The World Almanac and Book of Facts* 1992 (New York: Scripps Howard Co., 1991), page 311.

23. Earl D. Wilson, *Sexual Sanity* (Downers Grove, IL: InterVarsity, 1984), pages 18-19.

Chapter Four: The Warrior — *Gibbor*

1. This story is told by Terrance O'Connor. During a session with Robert Bly, Bly told a man to take his sword and symbolically kill his father, but the man refused, saying he would break his sword first. Bly responded by saying, "But what is man without his sword?" Cited in Keith Thompson, ed., *To Be a Man: In Search of the Deep Masculine* (Los Angeles: Jeremy P. Tarcher, 1991), page 245.

2. See Scott Alexander, *Rhinoceros Success* (Laguna Hills, CA: The Rhino Press, 1980), pages 9-24. This clever book, written and published by a business entrepreneur, is the classic statement of the modern American businessperson as warrior.

3. Robert Bly, *Iron John* (Reading, MA: Addison-Wesley, 1990), page 146.

4. Warren Farrell, *Why Men Are the Way They Are* (New York: Berkley Books, 1986), page 19.

5. Willard Gaylin, *The Male Ego* (New York: Viking Penguin, 1992), page 56.

6. Bly, page 156.

7. Patrick Arnold, *Wildmen, Warriors and Kings* (New York: Crossroad, 1991), pages 98-111; and Sam Keen, *Fire in the Belly* (New York: Bantam Books, 1991), pages 93-96.
8. Arnold, page 101.
9. Bly, page 165.
10. See Brown, Driver, and Briggs, *A Hebrew and English Lexicon of the Old Testament*; and G. Johannes Botterwick and Helmer Ringgren, ed., *Theological Dictionary of the Old Testament*, vol. 2 (Grand Rapids: Eerdmans, 1974), pages 367-368.
11. Deborah Tannen, *You Just Don't Understand* (New York: Ballantine Books, 1990), pages 24-25.
12. Robert Moore, *King, Warrior, Magician, Lover* (San Francisco: Harper, 1990), pages 75-95.
13. *The World Almanac and Book of Facts* 1992 (New York: Scripps Howard Co., 1991), pages 311-312.
14. Arnold, page 106.
15. Quoted in J. Glenn Gray, "The Enduring Appeals of Battle," in Thompson, pages 234-235.
16. Interview commented on by John Friel in his book, *The Grown-up Man* (Deerfield Beach, FL: Health Communications Inc., 1991), page 59.
17. Bly, page 171.

Chapter Five: The Wounded Male—*Enosh*

1. Robert Bly, *Iron John* (Reading, MA: Addison-Wesley, 1990), page 27.
2. Sam Keen, *Fire in the Belly* (New York: Bantam Books, 1991), page 46.
3. Robert A. Johnson, *He: Understanding Male Psychology* (New York: Harper and Row, 1974), page 10.
4. C. G. Jung, *Aspects of the Masculine* (Princeton, NJ: Princeton University Press, 1989), page 11.
5. Robert Fisher, *The Knight in Rusty Armor* (North Hollywood, CA: A Marcia Grad Publication, Wilshire Book Company, 1987), page 5.
6. Keen, page 31.

7. From the Akkadian root *enesu*, "to be weak." See G. Johannes Botterwick and Helmer Ringgren, ed., *Theological Dictionary of the Old Testament*, vol. 1 (Grand Rapids: Eerdmans, 1974), pages 345-348.

8. William Holladay, ed., *A Concise Hebrew and Aramaic Lexicon of the Old Testament* (Grand Rapids: Eerdmans, 1971), page 22; and S. R. Driver and Charles A. Briggs, *A Hebrew and English Lexicon of the Old Testament* (London: Oxford Press, 1907), page 60.

9. Philip Yancey, *Disappointment with God* (Grand Rapids: Zondervan, 1988), page 253.

10. Ted Dobson, "Healing the Tear in the Masculine Soul," *SCRC Vision*, April 1985.

11. Daniel J. Levinson, *The Seasons of a Man's Life* (New York: Ballantine Books, 1978), page 215.

12. Joe Tanenbaum notes, "A man's interaction in the world is through the physical or intellectual modes . . . men interpret the physical reality first . . . men express feelings through the body (physical)." Tanenbaum, *Male and Female Realities* (Sugarland, TX: Candle Publishing, 1989), pages 60-61; and Deborah Tannen says that women use language to maintain the network of connections while men use language to maintain hierarchy and being an individual in the social order. Tannen, *You Just Don't Understand* (New York: Ballantine Books, 1990), page 25.

13. Keen, page 41.

14. Gordon Dalbey, *Healing of the Masculine Soul* (Waco, TX: Word, 1988), page 52.

15. Quoted in Keith Thompson, ed., *To Be a Man: In Search of the Deep Masculine* (Los Angeles: Jeremy P. Tarcher, 1991), page 66.

16. Yancey, pages 248, 252.

17. George Gilder, *Men and Marriage* (Gretna, LA: Pelican Publishing, 1986), pages 109-110.

18. Gilder, page 27.

19. Lewis B. Puller, *Fortunate Son: The Healing of a Vietnam Vet* (New York: Grove Weidenfelf, 1991), pages 368-369.

Chapter Six: The Mature Man—*Ish*

1. Brown, Driver, and Briggs, *Hebrew and English Lexicon of the Old Testament* (Oxford, Great Britain: Oxford at the Clarendon Press, 1907), page 35.
2. William Holladay, ed., *A Concise Hebrew and Aramaic Lexicon of the Old Testament* (Grand Rapids: Eerdmans, 1971), page 13.
3. G. Johannes Botterwick and Helmer Ringgren, ed., *Theological Dictionary of the Old Testament*, vol. 1 (Grand Rapids: Eerdmans, 1974), page 222.
4. John Friel, *The Grown-up Man* (Deerfield Beach, FL: Health Communications Inc., 1991), page 14.
5. Friel, page 14.
6. Friel, pages 188-190.
7. Sam Keen, *Fire in the Belly* (New York: Bantam Books, 1991), page 23.
8. Daniel Levinson, *Seasons of a Man's Life* (New York: Ballantine Books, 1978), page 242.
9. Francois Duc de La Rochefoucauld, *Reflections; or Sentences and Moral Maxims*, listed in *Bartlett's Familiar Quotations* (Boston: Little, Brown, 1980), page 292.
10. Levinson, pages 240-241.
11. Levinson, page 249.
12. Elton Trueblood, *Alternative to Futility* (New York: Harper and Brothers, 1948), page 15.
13. J. H. Newman, *Meditations and Devotions* (Wheathampstead, Hertfordshire: Anthony Clarke Books, 1964), pages 6-7.
14. See Botterwick and Ringgren, vol. 1, pages 226-229.
15. Levinson, page 251.
16. Robert Frost, "The Road Not Taken," in *The Poetry of Robert Frost*, Edward Connery Lathem, ed. (New York: Holt, Rinehart and Winston, 1969).

Chapter Seven: The Sage—*Zaken*

1. Taken from Robert Lacy, *The Kingdom: Arabia and the House of Saud* (New York: Avon Books, 1981), page 18.

2. Brown, Driver, and Briggs, *Hebrew and English Lexicon of the Old Testament* (Oxford, Great Britain: Oxford at the Clarendon Press, 1907), page 278.
3. William Holladay, ed., *A Concise Hebrew and Aramaic Lexicon of the Old Testament* (Grand Rapids: Eerdmans, 1971), page 91.
4. One year after my father's retirement as a corporate executive, he and my mother visited a church for the first time. The same week, they got a call from the pastor asking if my father could park cars on Sunday! Need I say, they never went back.
5. G. Johannes Botterwick and Helmer Ringgren, ed., *Theological Dictionary of the Old Testament*, vol. 4 (Grand Rapids: Eerdmans, 1974), pages 122-131.
6. Daniel J. Levinson, "Late Adulthood," in Keith Thompson, ed., *To Be a Man: In Search of the Deep Masculine* (Los Angeles: Jeremy P. Tarcher, 1991), page 261.
7. For examples see Paul Stanley and Robert Clinton, *Connecting: The Mentoring Relationships You Need to Succeed in Life* (Colorado Springs, CO: NavPress, 1992).
8. From materials made available to Seminary of the East by The Uncommon Individual Foundation, Radnor, Pennsylvania, in 1990-1992.
9. Daniel J. Levinson, *Seasons of a Man's Life* (New York: Ballantine Books, 1978), pages 251, 253.

Chapter Eight: A New Male Journey
1. See Kenneth Stokes, ed., *Faith Development in the Adult Life Cycle* (New York: W. H. Sadlier Co., 1982) for an overview of this question.
2. Nikolai Gogol, *Dead Souls*, quoted in *Bartlett's Familiar Quotations* (Boston: Little, Brown, 1980), page 518.

Author

◆

Robert Hicks's masculine journey has taken him down many roads. As an educator, Dr. Hicks is professor of Pastoral Theology at the Seminary of the East in Philadelphia. As a counselor, he was cofounder of Life Counseling Services, located in the Philadelphia area. As a chaplain in the Air National Guard, he serves an A-10 fighter group. As a communicator, he has authored *Uneasy Manhood* (Nelson, 1991), which deals with men's issues, *Returning Home* (Revell, 1991), in response to the Gulf War, and *Failure to Scream* (Nelson, 1993), a well-researched look at post-traumatic stress disorder. He holds degrees in psychology, theology, and family studies and has pursued post-doctoral work in religious studies (Villanova University).

In 1985, Dr. Hicks was honored with the American Legion nomination for "Chaplain of the Year," an award presented by President Reagan for Dr. Hicks's work with the families and survivors of the Delta 191 crash at Dallas–Ft. Worth Airport.

Dr. Hicks resides in Berwyn, Pennsylvania, a Philadelphia suburb, with his wife, Cinny, two children, and one dog. He also has one married daughter.

About Promise Keepers

◆────────────◆

Promise Keepers is an organization dedicated to motivating men toward greater strength and Christlike masculinity.

Promise Keepers sponsors men's conferences in regional locations and various churches around the country. The annual Promise Keepers National Men's Conference is held each July in Boulder, Colorado.

Promise Keepers seeks to be a supply line to the local church, helping to encourage and assist pastors and ministry leaders in calling men to an accountable relationship with Jesus Christ and with one another. Promise Keepers wants to provide men's materials (like this book) as well as seminars and the annual conference to emphasize the godly conviction, integrity, and action each of us needs.

Please join us in helping one another be the kind of men God wants us to be. Write or call our offices today.

Promise Keepers
P.O. Box 18376
Boulder, CO 80308

1-800-228-3100
or
1-303-421-2800